SIGMUND FREUD

Liz Gogerly

W

FRANKLIN WATTS
LONDON•SYDNEY

Map Ian Thompson
Designer Steve Prosser
Editor Constance Novis
Art Director Jonathan Hair
Editor-in-Chief John C. Miles
Picture Research Susan Mennell

Consultant Eileen Yeo
Professor of Social and Cultural
History, University of Strathclyde

First published in 2003
by Franklin Watts
96 Leonard Street
London
EC2A 4XD

Franklin Watts Australia
45-51 Huntley Street
Alexandria
NSW 2015

ISBN 0 7496 4693 4

A CIP catalogue record
for this book is available
from the British Library.

Printed in Hong Kong/China

Picture credits
Front and back cover images: AKG

AKG pp. 2, 3, 5, 6, 9, 10, 27, 30, 33,
36, 38, 57, 62, 69, 73, 78, 83, 85, 87,
91, 93, 95, 97, 99, 101
Mary Evans Picture Library pp. 14, 18,
20, 22, 24-25, 42, 45, 47, 48, 52, 58,
65, 66, 76, 89
Topham Picturepoint pp. 14, 42, 48,
52, 76

Sigmund Freud
1856–1939

Contents

Introduction

More than one hundred years ago an unknown Viennese doctor called Sigmund Freud heard about the strange case of a young woman suffering from a peculiar selection of symptoms.

The 21-year-old woman had a cough that wouldn't go away, then suffered from loss of feeling in her hands and feet. Eventually she began to experience difficulties with her speech. Her doctor could find no physical reason for her illness, so he suggested that she was hysterical. The patient had recently been tending her sick father. Soon afterwards, when he died, her symptoms became so bad that she began to experience terrible hallucinations and threatened to commit suicide. The case was not that unusual, but how could she be cured? At this time the nature of the human mind was a mystery, and nobody knew how to cure hysteria.

The woman in question had been the patient of Freud's close friend, Dr Joseph Breuer. In time Breuer had noticed that his patient seemed to improve when she talked about herself. Sometimes she went into a trance and seemed to talk nonsense but, as if by magic, one of the symptoms might disappear. Many years later, when he heard about this case, Freud began to think that hysteria might be caused by something that had happened in a person's past. He believed that by repressing, or holding in, painful memories a person might become ill. The remedy was to talk through and analyze what had happened long ago. By doing this, the negative feelings produced by the memories could be resolved and the person would be cured. In 1895 Breuer and Freud published a book called *Studies in Hysteria*. It laid down the foundations for a new science and therapy called psychoanalysis.

Revolution of the mind

Psychoanalysis is a method of understanding how someone's mind works. By asking a person questions to

▶ *A portrait photograph of Sigmund Freud with his habitual cigar, taken in 1921.*

encourage them to talk about themselves and examining their answers, the psychoanalyst can find patterns in that person's way of thinking.

Freud is known as the "father of psychoanalysis". It is his pioneering work that gave us the first idea of how the mind worked. Until Freud people did not think that we possessed an unconscious mind that was capable of affecting our behaviour. They did not realize that dreams, or everyday slips of the tongues (which later came to be known as "Freudian slips"), could help us to understand ourselves, and solve our problems. Nobody had suggested that sexuality, and particularly childhood sexuality, might play an important part in a person's development.

Psychoanalysis has quite literally revolutionized the way people think about themselves. As with any new ideas, Freud's theories and techniques were often criticized. Today, however, some of his ideas are so much a part of the way we think that it is hard to imagine a time when people found his theories shocking or simply ridiculous.

◀ *Another portrait of Freud, taken in Vienna in 1926.*

The early years

The lasting image of Sigmund Freud is of a white-haired man with a neatly trimmed beard, a conservative suit, a cigar in his hand and a dark stare that seems to look straight through you in an all-knowing way.

It is hard to believe that this same eminent doctor came from a poor immigrant Jewish family. Sigismund Scholomo (Freud changed his name to Sigmund years later when he entered the University of Vienna) was born on 6 May 1856 in Freiburg, a small town in Moravia. At that time the region was part of the Austro-Hungarian Empire, but Moravia now is part of the Czech Republic.

Freud's father Jacob Freud had already been married three times when Sigmund was born. Jacob also had two grown-up sons, Emanuel and Philipp. Sigmund's mother Amalia was twenty years younger than her 45-year-old husband and younger than his sons. As a child, Freud often thought his youthful, good-looking mother was better suited to his half-brother Philipp, who was nearer to his mother's age than his father's. A family with such large age gaps presented other confusions, too. One of Freud's dearest childhood friends was his nephew, John, who was the son of his elder brother, Emanuel. However, it must have felt strange for Sigmund to be uncle to a child who was a year older than him. Did such a complicated family structure trigger Freud's interest in human relationships, and in turn his fascination with the effects of those relationships upon the mind? We'll never know for sure.

Life in Vienna

When Sigmund was born Jacob was working as a wool merchant, earning just enough to rent one room above a blacksmith's shop. Not much is known about Freud's childhood. In 1858 his sister Anna was born. Once again, Freud was confused; was the baby something to do with his brother Philipp? In 1859 the

▶ *A portrait of Sigmund or "Sigi" aged eight, in 1864, with his father Jacob Freud.*

Freuds moved briefly to Germany before settling in Vienna, the capital city of Austria. For centuries Vienna had been a popular destination for Jews fleeing from persecution in other parts of Europe. By 1860 there were 15,000 Jews living in Vienna. Over half of them lived in poor run-down accommodation in a district to the northeast of the city called Leopoldstadt. The Freuds were just one of many Jewish families struggling to make ends meet in what became a crowded ghetto. Jacob tried to provide for his family but a steady stream of births didn't make life easy. Between the years 1860 and 1866 four girls (Rosa, Marie, Adolfine, Pauline) and a boy (Alexander) were born. By now Emanuel and Philipp had emigrated to Manchester, England. It's not known how Jacob supported his young family but it is believed his elder sons might have helped out.

The favourite child

Of all their children, Amalia and Jacob believed that Sigmund, or "Sigi" as he was

◀ *This formal portrait shows Sigmund Freud with his mother Amalia. It was taken in 1872, when Sigmund was 16.*

affectionately known, was destined for higher things. A story that Amalia liked to tell was how an old peasant woman had told her that her beloved son would become "a great man". Years later, when Freud was about twelve, a poet in a café predicted that Sigmund would become a government minister.

The Freuds did their best to ensure their son received a good education. He went to a private Jewish school until he was nine, then to the local state-run high school. Sigmund's parents hoped that their studious and rather confident son would go on to study law and support the family. Even though their living conditions were cramped, they always made sure that Sigmund had a room of his own in which to study. It must have been difficult for the other children in the family, but Sigmund seemed to make few concessions for their sacrifices on his behalf. When he was ten he complained about his sister Anna's piano lessons. The piano was quickly removed so "Sigi" could study in peace. If he found Anna reading what were considered by some to be unsuitable books, he complained to his parents and the books were immediately taken away.

The serious student

Freud was an outstanding student who was nearly always top of his class. In the final year at school he had his first lesson in love too. This was a brief and innocent flirtation with one of his schoolfriend's sisters. His "affair" with Gisela Fluss, whom he had met while on holiday in Freiberg, was short, sweet and probably not much more than a boy's first crush. In 1873 Freud graduated from high school with distinction. By now he wanted to study natural science, or zoology, rather than law. He had been partly influenced by the work of Charles Darwin, the English naturalist and the man who originated the theory of evolution by natural selection. Freud, however, was more interested in studying the nature, or behaviour, of humans.

In 1873 the Freuds scraped together enough money to send their favourite son to the University of Vienna to study medicine. Freud, who was just seventeen, threw himself into work, often staying up until two in the morning reading for his lectures; but he soon discovered that university life had its downside too. At that time anti-Semitic feeling was on the rise in Vienna. This prejudice was even present at the university. Although Freud wasn't a practising Jew (he had decided he was an atheist), the atmosphere made him uncomfortable and he hoped one day to leave Vienna.

In 1875, during his university holiday, Freud visited his brothers in Manchester, England. At that time, England was the centre of a large empire, and a place where ideas, particularly in science and medicine, flourished. Freud had longed to visit England. He came away determined that he would set up a medical practice there one day.

When Freud returned to Vienna he was selected by the university to research

From the law to nature

"Now I can speak freely. When I lift the veil of secrecy, will you not be disappointed? Well let's see. I have decided to be a Natural Scientist and herewith release you from the promise to let me conduct all your law-suits. It is no longer needed. I shall gain insight into the age-old dossiers of Nature, perhaps even eavesdrop on her eternal processes, and share my findings with anyone who wants to learn."
Freud in a letter to his friend Emil Fluss on 1 May 1873

EUROPE in 1900
Showing cities mentioned in this book

marine biology in Trieste in northern Italy. Freud's serious young mind was given a jolt in Italy as he witnessed a culture more hot-blooded than his own. In letters home he wrote about the Italian women, and their make-up and clothing, of which he wasn't sure he approved. Meanwhile the research he conducted was into the sex organs of eels. Although Freud didn't enjoy cutting open hundreds of dead eels, the task gave him a good, solid grounding in scientific research and taught him the importance of close observation of a subject.

The nervous system

Upon his return to Vienna, Freud studied under the Professor of Physiology, Ernst Wilhelm von Brücke. Brücke, who would

become a father-figure to Freud, was already famous in the scientific world and Freud hoped that a little of the great professor's genius would rub off on him. Freud's work began by observing the nervous systems of fish and other marine animals. He spent long hours stooped over microscopes looking for minute details that would help explain more about their nervous systems. It was hard, exacting work but he was eventually rewarded with the opportunity to research the thing that interested him most – the human nervous system. Freud studied at the university for eight years and graduated as a Doctor of Medicine in 1881.

Although he was badly paid Freud stayed on at the university and continued with his research. He was driven by his ambition to discover something new. At the back of his mind, however, he worried that he didn't have it in him to be a success.

Falling in love

Freud's early work into the nervous system would be important to him, but by spring 1882 he had given up research at the university to pursue a goal much closer to his heart. He had fallen deeply in love with an attractive young Jewish girl called Martha Bernays. Problems soon arose because Martha came from a more distinguished family than the Freuds. Her family were practising Jews too, whereas Freud had long since given up his religion.

However, perhaps the most unsuitable attribute of the young Freud was his lack of money to support Martha. The only way for Freud to provide for her was to become a doctor. Three weeks after meeting Martha, Freud took a job at the General Hospital in Vienna. Just over a month later, Freud asked Martha to be his wife. Martha had other suitors but she wanted to marry Freud. She accepted his proposal but they decided to keep their engagement a secret until he became more established.

◄ *Martha Bernays, with whom Freud fell in love and was later to marry.*

The young professional

The next three years seemed to drag on forever for the love-struck young doctor, as he moved around departments at the hospital searching for an area in which to specialize.

Freud was also working part-time under the great brain anatomist Theodor Meynert at the Institute of Cerebral Anatomy. The decision about his future became more and more difficult to make. Sometimes he thought about becoming a dermatologist and emigrating to America where he could set up his own practice. Other times he wondered about a career in neurology and the scientific study of nerve systems.

While he fretted about his career he pined for Martha whom he rarely saw, as she now lived near Hamburg in Germany. The couple wrote to each other daily – Martha's letters were modest and tame, in keeping with a young woman of those times, but Freud's letters were romantic and revealed a man frustrated in his career and his personal life. He longed to consummate the marriage, and tormented himself with the thought Martha might be with somebody else. It was during this time that Freud's lifelong addiction to smoking cigars began. "Smoking is indispensable if one has nothing to kiss," he once wrote to Martha, in a dramatic fashion that would be so out of character in later life.

"The magical substance"

The late nineteenth century was an exciting time to be involved in science or medicine. Discoveries about the human body and cures for illnesses were the kind of stories that hit the front pages of newspapers. The 1880s was a particularly interesting decade. Frenchman Louis Pasteur discovered vaccines for anthrax and rabies, while German scientist Robert Koch discovered the germ that caused tuberculosis. Freud read about these massive breakthroughs in medicine, and in

April 1884 believed he might be on the verge of a ground-breaking discovery of his own. If this was the case, then his marriage to Martha could be brought forward – and that, more than anything else at the time, obsessed Freud.

In the course of his research Freud had come across a drug that was derived from the leaves of the coca plant; the drug was called cocaine, and very little was known about it. Freud had read about Peruvians who chewed on coca leaves to give themselves a lift. He'd also read about German soldiers who had taken cocaine to keep them going for longer periods of time. Freud hoped that the drug might cure depression, or even heart disease. He also meant to test it out as a possible cure for morphine addiction. Morphine is a drug that is used medicinally to relieve pain, but it is highly addictive, and, if taken in large quantities, can kill.

Freud's first willing candidate to test the drug was his friend Ernst von Fleischl-Marxow, who had become dependent on morphine following an infection. Freud also took cocaine himself, and found that it helped with headaches and indigestion, as well as giving him a lift in stressful situations. Freud had such faith in the drug he nicknamed it "the magical substance" and would even send small amounts to Martha, which he told her in one of his letters would "make her strong and give her cheeks a red colour".

Freud published his findings in July 1884 in a paper called "On Coca". Unfortunately his claims for cocaine would be premature. Fleischl-Marxow became addicted to cocaine, and another doctor discovered a more effective use for the drug. In 1884 Dr Carl Koller discovered that cocaine could be used as a local anaesthetic during eye surgery. For years afterwards the drug often served as an anaesthetic. Freud had overlooked the most impressive property of the drug and the whole episode must have been rather embarrassing. Nevertheless, Freud continued to use cocaine off and on for many years, without becoming addicted.

His dented ego also bounced back, and in 1885 he told Martha that he had destroyed his papers on science and medicine from the previous 14 years. In a letter he told her: "Let the biographers labour and toil, we won't make it too easy for them." Sigmund Freud obviously still had a belief that he would one day be famous.

▲ Medical science advanced rapidly in the late nineteenth century. This print shows the French scientist Louis Pasteur, who developed vaccines for both anthrax and rabies, in his laboratory in 1885.

Some important discoveries in medicine and science in the late nineteenth century

- **1847** American dentist WTG Morton uses ether as an anaesthetic for the first time
- **1859** Charles Darwin's *The Origin of Species* is published
- **1864** Louis Pasteur discovers that micro-organisms in air cause milk to go sour and presents his germ theory
- **1865** Sir Joseph Lister discovers that antiseptics prevent the formation of germs
- **1868** John W Hyatt produces plastic (celluloid); Georges Leclanche patents the dry cell battery
- **1876** Alexander Graham Bell invents the telephone; Nikolaus Otto designs the internal combustion engine
- **1877** Thomas Edison invents the phonograph
- **1880** Louis Pasteur discovers streptococcus bacteria
- **1881** Louis Pasteur discovers a vaccination against anthrax
- **1882** Robert Koch discovers the bacteria that causes tuberculosis
- **1883** Thomas Edison and Joseph Swan produce the carbon-filament light
- **1885** Louis Pasteur uses the rabies vaccine for the first time; Carl Benz and Gottlieb Daimler construct the first motor car
- **1895** Wilhelm Roentgen discovers X-rays; Kodak produces the first pocket camera
- **1898** Marie Curie discovers radium and radioactivity; the first commercial wireless telegram is transmitted
- **1900** Blood groups are discovered by Karl Landsteiner

Diseases of the mind

In the 1880s the world still had much to learn about the brain and the workings of the mind. At this time psychology, or the study of human behaviour, was fairly new in the UK and the USA, while in Europe the science of neurology and psychology were treated as one, as they both involved the brain. Mental disorders were not usually treated as serious illnesses. Often sufferers were dealt with as if they were putting the symptoms on, and in most cases the patient was simply hidden away, their existence not openly discussed. At that time, anyone unfortunate enough to be considered mad or hysterical was likely to be committed to a mental asylum or a madhouse. These overcrowded places were usually little more than prisons where patients were locked up and restrained,

and nobody tried to understand the causes of their problems.

Psychiatry, or the study of mental diseases, was also in its infancy. In autumn 1884 Freud turned his attentions towards this unexplored area of research. He was particularly interested in the work carried out by the famous French neurologist, Jean-Martin Charcot, who had been researching neuroses and hysteria at the Salpêtrière Hospital in Paris. Charcot had attempted to learn more about hysteria and had tried to show that hysteria was not caused by the imagination, as was the common belief at the time. He discovered that hysteria manifested itself in many ways, from convulsions to loss of control over bodily functions or even double vision and colour blindness. He also found that hysterical patients had different psychological symptoms such as depression, mood swings or irritability. Charcot had also tried to destroy the myth that only women could suffer from the condition. He'd found that men were less likely to become hysterical but there was still a chance they could. This was pioneering work and Freud realized that there were amazing possibilities within this fascinating field.

In October 1885 Freud visited Paris for the first time. He spent six months with Charcot, studying hysteria. The prospect of being in Paris had been so exciting but the reality was somewhat different. Freud didn't earn much money so he couldn't afford trips to the theatre or shows. Instead he strolled through the bustling streets of the capital, looking at the magnificent architecture and taking in the atmosphere. Freud often felt lonely in Paris. As well as having difficulties with the French language, he found himself disapproving of what he considered to be the vulgarity of the women. Fortunately,

Terms used by psychoanalysts and psychologists

●**neurosis:** Originally described a disease of the nerves but came to mean the mild personality disorders that can interfere with the ability to live a normal life. Neuroses can be divided into **hysteria, anxiety** and **obsessive-compulsive disorders**. These disorders can be cured by psychoanalysis.

●**hysteria:** The physical symptom of neurosis, this can include paralysis, headaches and sleeplessness.

●**anxiety:** Includes conditions like phobias and panic attacks.

●**obsessive-compulsive disorders:** Obsessions are ideas that are abnormal and intrude upon a person's ability to live a normal life. Symptoms of obsessive-compulsive disorders include performing a ritual over and over again, such as washing one's hands.

●**psychosis:** Term for severe mental illnesses where it has become impossible for the patient to separate fantasy from reality. Psychoses include schizophrenia, manic depression and paranoia. These illnesses cannot be cured by psychoanalysis.

●**paranoia:** A mental disorder where a patient suffers from delusions. This might lead them to believe that they're being followed by a stranger, or that somebody loves them from a distance.

●**manic depression:** A mental disorder where the patient alternates between depression and mania (great excitement characterized by speaking too quickly or becoming violent).

●**schizophrenia:** A mental disorder where the patient has a breakdown in the relation between thoughts, feelings and actions. Most patients experience delusions and hallucinations, which lead to a change in personality.

he gained important insights into the nature of hysteria, and Charcot made a huge impression upon him. "Charcot," he wrote, "who is one of the greatest physicians, a genius and a sober man, simply uproots my views and intentions. After some lectures I walk away as from Notre Dame, with a new perception of perfection."

Charcot was a great showman who introduced Freud to hypnotism as a means of curing hysteria. At this time many people considered hypnotism to be

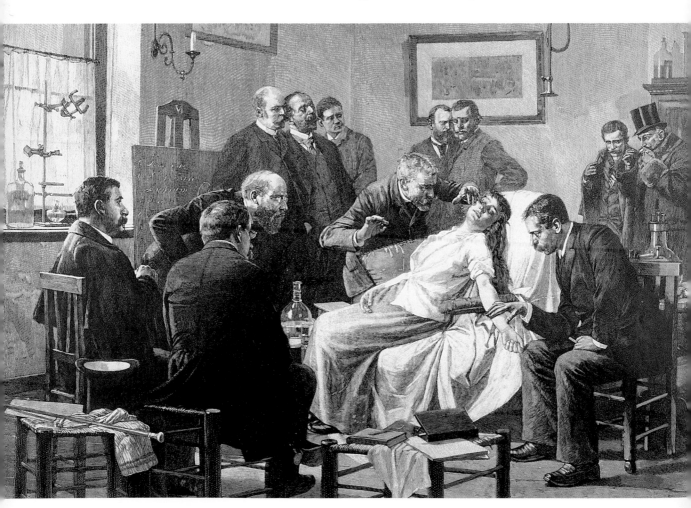

▼ *German doctors observe a demonstration of hypnosis on a female patient in about 1890.*

Different branches of medicine and psychology

- **neurology**: The scientific study of the nervous system.
- **psychology**: The scientific study of the human mind; also the science of behaviour. Psychoanalysis is a branch of psychology.
- **psychiatry:** The branch of medicine that treats mental illness or psychosis. Techniques include electro-shock therapy and certain drugs.
- **psychoanalysis:** The theory and therapeutic treatment of neuroses. The patient is helped to investigate their unconscious feelings and recognize their repressed fears and conflicts. Techniques Include the "talking cure" or as it is now known, "free association".

something for con men and cranks but Charcot had discovered something intriguing about hypnotism. He'd found that while people were being hypnotized they could be told to become paralyzed or made to do things they would never do when they were awake. He went on to discover that when hysterical people were hypnotized their symptoms could be removed or changed. This was one of the first serious attempts to find a therapy for hysteria, but there was still much more to discover about the human mind.

Freud's early career

When Freud returned to Vienna in spring 1886 he was still undecided about his future.

Freud considered moving abroad, possibly to England, the country he liked so much. He was almost certain that he wanted to set himself up as a nerve doctor who would deal with nervous or hysterical complaints, but he didn't feel ready yet. He took on a part-time appointment at a children's hospital, and for a while thought about specializing in children's nervous diseases. But at the back of his mind there was that nagging desperation to marry Martha. "Oh, my darling Marty, how poor we are!" he wrote in one of his love-letters, and soon it was obvious that the only way they could marry was if he had his own practice. That same spring Freud resigned

▶ *A view of Vienna in the 1880s taken from a tinted postcard.*

from the hospital, found two rooms near Vienna Town Hall and in April 1886 placed a notice in the local newspaper advertising for patients. Freud's practice opened at Easter 1886. Many of his first patients had been recommended to him by his colleagues. Most of these patients were neurotic women with symptoms like backache, headaches, loss of appetite, tiredness or sleeplessness. Although Freud found some of the cases boring, he experimented with hypnotism and learned something new from every person he treated. Some of his clients couldn't afford to pay him but the little money Freud did make allowed him to start planning his wedding.

Married life

On 13 September 1886, more than four years after they became engaged, Freud and Martha finally got married. They moved into a four-room apartment in a reasonably fashionable part of Vienna. We know so much about Freud's long engagement because hundreds of his love-letters to Martha still survive. In complete contrast, we know very little about the Freuds' personal life once they were married. Freud had been a jealous

fiancé. Perhaps, now that he and Martha were married, he jealously guarded their privacy instead. From the start, he handed the running of the household over to Martha but he was adamant that it should be non-religious. Martha, who had been brought up as a devout Jewish girl, could no longer light the Sabbath candles on a Friday night. She was upset by this situation, but like many young wives at that time, she did as she was told, and the two settled down to enjoy married life.

Within a few months Martha had organized their home, and given it the supreme orderliness that was characteristic of all their future houses. Martha was in many ways a typical *hausfrau* (housewife) who demanded punctuality and often scolded Freud for being messy. Freud, who had a dry sense of humour, found being told off by his young wife amusing and joked to Martha's sister, Minna, that he was henpecked. Life for the newlyweds should have been total bliss but money was a constant worry. Freud's practice got busier

▶ *This 1886 photograph shows Sigmund and Martha Freud shortly after their marriage.*

but he still didn't earn enough to pay the rent. On a few occasions he was forced to pawn (borrow money against) their gold watches to pay their bills.

Controversy

The situation wasn't helped because Freud's work was becoming more controversial. In October 1886 he gave his first lecture to the leading medical society in Vienna, the Viennese Physicians' Society. He dared to promote some of the theories about hysteria that had been introduced to him by Charcot.

His suggestion that hysteria wasn't an illness or disease was received with scepticism, but the very idea of men also suffering from hysteria was deemed by some older doctors to be preposterous. One of Freud's long-standing colleagues, Theodor Meynert, even challenged him to present a case of male hysteria to the society.

This kind of reaction made Freud realize that his work would take him further and further away from the world of established medicine. However, not even Freud himself could have imagined just how alienated from that world he would become in the future.

Important friends

Throughout his long career Freud took solace from close friendship with other doctors and psychologists. These relationships often gave him the support and confidence to continue with his work. One of the most influential friends in his early career was the physician Josef Breuer. Freud had met Breuer while he was still a student and had often turned to his older friend, who became another father-figure, when he needed money or advice. It had been Breuer who had told him about an interesting case of hysteria in a woman he had treated in 1880. The young woman was called Bertha Pappenheim but to protect her privacy the case had been named "The Case of Anna O", and is recognized as the first case of psychoanalysis. Even though Bertha was Breuer's patient, this case would become the basis for much of Freud's future work.

The case of Anna O

When Breuer met Bertha Pappenheim for the first time he described her as an intelligent, healthy 21-year-old. Healthy, that was, except for her strange symptoms that had started when she began nursing her sick father in 1880. At first, when her father had become ill, Bertha had been exhausted. Next she lost her appetite, then she developed a nervous cough and a squint. Subsequently, she had suffered from headaches, mood swings, hallucinations and even partial paralysis of her right arm and neck. Breuer had been summoned to help Bertha, and for a while she did seem to get better. But, by April 1881 when her father died, her symptoms had grown more alarming.

In the daytime she was plagued by violent hallucinations about black snakes, skulls and skeletons. In the evening she fell into a strange trance-like state when she spoke in half-sentences with no real meaning. Breuer visited the troubled young woman on a daily basis and listened to the stories that seemed to pour out of her. Sometimes her tales were happy, other times they were sad, but talking seemed to help Bertha recall feelings and emotions she'd forgotten she had. By talking, or "chimney sweeping" as she jokingly called it, some of her symptoms seemed to go away. One of Bertha's more bizarre symptoms had been a temporary fear of water; despite a raging thirst, she was unable to drink. Fortunately, during one of their "chimney-sweeping" sessions Bertha recalled her disgust at her English lady-companion who had allowed a dog to drink out of her glass. By remembering the incident Bertha's phobia about water was somehow banished or "talked away".

The key

In 1882 Breuer told Freud about this fascinating case, and the success of the technique he'd named the "cathartic method". At the time Freud had been influenced by Charcot and pursued hypnotism instead. After setting up his own practice Freud began looking for a more satisfactory way of treating his patients than hypnotism. In 1885 Breuer told Freud more about the Anna O case. At the end of Breuer's association with Bertha she had seemed to become dependent upon him and their sessions. Then, as her symptoms disappeared and the treatment drew to a close, she had a dramatic relapse. In their final session, Bertha had been been found writhing around with stomach pains. She claimed they were caused by the child that she was carrying – Breuer's child! Bertha's pregnancy was pure fantasy, but the mere suggestion was so scandalous that Breuer dropped the case immediately. When

Freud heard these extra details, his mind raced with possibilities. Bertha had obviously fallen in love with Breuer – was this something that needed to be questioned and investigated further? Could it have been that Bertha's sexuality was part of the problem?

At that time, just the mention of the word sexuality caused most "respectable" people to throw up their hands in horror. Perhaps because he was so closely involved in the case, Breuer chose to distance himself from such radical ideas. Freud, on the other hand, believed that he had been handed a clue to the solution of a significant problem.

◀ *Bertha Pappenheim (1859–1936), as depicted on a German postage stamp of 1954. "Helper of Mankind" read the words on the right.*

The gateway to the unconscious

In October 1887 the Freuds had their first child, a daughter they named Mathilde, after Breuer's wife.

Freud enjoyed being a father, and parenthood would keep him very busy in the years to come – so much so that he did not do much to further his theories about sexuality and hysteria. By 1895 the voices of young children often filled the Freud home. Three boys, Martin, Oliver and Ernst, and two more girls, Sophie and Anna, completed the family. Having so many children put great strain on Martha who, it seemed, was always either pregnant or recovering from childbirth. It presented frustrations of a different kind to Freud, who at just 39 considered himself to be middle-aged. He adored his family but he often felt depressed.

Perhaps this depression had more to do with his relationship with Martha. The Freuds still loved one another, but fear of getting Martha pregnant again meant that they had practically stopped having sex. Although there were forms of contraception available, such as condoms, Freud did not believe in them.

At that time most people disagreed with birth control on moral grounds, but Freud strongly believed that "holding back" or barrier methods like the condom could cause neurosis or psychological problems. In the nineteenth century it was not unusual for husbands in this position to take a mistress, but there is little evidence that Freud did so. Perhaps it could be said that the lack of sex in his own life made Freud more interested in trying to understand other people's sexuality.

New techniques

While Freud came to terms with his responsibilities as a family man his practice grew. Making a living was a priority, but discovering new methods of

▶ *A photograph of Berggasse 19, Vienna, where Freud lived and worked from 1891 to 1938.*

treating his patients was a driving force as well. For a while Freud followed the development of new electrical devices for the treatment of mental illness. Some doctors claimed that passing electricity through a patient could cure them of many kinds of neuroses. Before long, however, Freud dismissed this technique, calling it a "construction of fantasy".

In 1891 the Freuds moved to another apartment at Berggasse 19 in Vienna. This was their home for the next 47 years, and it would become the address that we most associate with Freud and his pioneering work as a psychoanalyst.

When he arrived at Berggasse Freud was mainly using hypnotism to cure his patients but he still did not know if it really worked. By the early 1890s Freud was also dabbling in Breuer's "talking cure" or cathartic method. Between 1892 and 1896 Freud had adapted the method so that his patients now lay on a couch while he pressed his hand to their forehead. As he applied pressure, Freud told his patients to think of any words that came into their head. To start with they just uttered random words, but gradually the words would trigger memories. This technique is now known as free association. Freud would listen patiently as they told him snippets about their lives. As their memories unravelled, Freud found that many people told him things that perhaps they had never intended to tell – or even things they had forgotten. Freud believed that it was those details that were important, and by releasing these memories and interpreting them, the patient could be cured.

Early cases

While Freud experimented with his patients on the couch, he persuaded his friend Breuer to work with him on a book. *Studies in Hysteria* would contain many of Freud's early cases, some of which were recorded in minute detail, and it reveals how Freud experimented with different techniques as he went along. They also show how eloquent and convincing Freud's style of writing could be. Freud likened the case studies to stories, but this was something that critics would later seize on – were Freud's case studies more fiction than fact? The first of these cases was Emmy von N., the middle-aged widow of a rich Russian-Swiss industrialist. Her real name was Fanny Moser and, like Bertha

Pappenheim of the Anna O case, she had various symptoms including depression, hallucinations, insomnia, and strange aches and pains. To start with Freud recommended massage and rest, but eventually he tried hypnotism.

Fanny responded well to hypnotism but gradually Freud found that the sessions where he listened to her talk were the most effective. It was through Fanny that Freud discovered that certain words could trigger stories or memories, the telling of which would help to cure the patient.

Another early case was that of Katharina, real name Aurelia Kronich, the eighteen-year-old daughter of an innkeeper that Freud had met on a mountain walk. The interlude had only lasted an afternoon but in that time the young woman had told Freud about her bouts of breathlessness, and the "awful face" that she kept seeing in her head. Freud recognized that the girl was suffering from panic attacks and he listened to her story in the hope that he would discover the root of her illness. This case was interesting because it was the first time that Freud traced symptoms back to something sexual that had happened in childhood. In this particular case, Aurelia's hysteria had been caused by the sexual advances of her own father.

Studies in Hysteria

When *Studies in Hysteria* was published in 1895 it summarized all that Freud and Breuer had discovered about hysteria so far. They concluded that hysterics suffered from painful "reminiscences" or memories. Over time, these memories did not go away, rather they were repressed, and remained in the unconscious mind. As these bad memories were not expressed they built up, eventually showing up as physical symptoms like panic attacks or phobias. However, these symptoms would disappear if the repressed memories or emotions were released. These were new, revolutionary ideas – ideas that would evolve into psychoanalysis – but sadly Breuer was never credited in the same way as Freud. Freud had persuaded Breuer, much against his will, to include the case of Anna O in the book.

Increasingly, Breuer did not like the connection that Freud was making between sexuality and hysteria. He felt that Freud was using the case of Anna O as evidence of his theories about

sexuality. Sadly, the old friends fell out in 1894 before the book was even published.

New friends

While Freud sought to understand other people, he battled to understand himself. He'd had periods of depression for years, but from 1893 he began to suffer from panic attacks, and suspected that he had heart problems. He was on the brink of making major discoveries about hysteria but he was working very much on his own. Sometimes he must have felt rather frightened but he found comfort in his family and friendships.

In 1894 – with Breuer out of his life – he might well have felt even more isolated had he not, in 1887, met Dr Wilhelm Fliess. Fliess was an ear, nose and throat specialist from Berlin. The nineteenth century had its fair share of medical geniuses and cranks. Fliess would turn out to be a mad doctor who believed that the nose was the most important organ in the body and that it influenced health and sexuality.

It seems that his outlandish beliefs were accepted by Freud who even allowed Fliess to operate on his nose to cure his heart problem. For years Fliess was an important sounding board for Freud, and between 1887 and 1902 there was a constant stream of letters between the two friends. In his letters to Fliess, Freud was at his most open and human. He was as likely to write about his delight at his children growing up as discuss his new theories about hysteria.

An interior view of Freud's consulting room in the apartment at Berggasse 19, showing the famous couch.

Extracts from Freud's letters to his friend, Wilhelm Fliess

"I am still all mixed up. I am almost certain that I have solved the riddles of hysteria and obsessional neurosis with the formulas of infantile sexual shock and sexual pleasure, and I am equally certain that both neuroses are, in general, curable ... this gives me a faint joy – for having lived some forty years not quite in vain ..."

"I am actually not at all a man of science, not an observer, not an experimenter, not a thinker. I am by temperament nothing but a *conquistador* – an adventurer, if you want it translated – with all the curiosity, daring and tenacity characteristic of a man of this sort."

▲ Freud (left) and his friend, the German ear, nose and throat doctor Wilhelm Fliess in a photograph taken in about 1890. The two men corresponded regularly until 1902.

These letters have become an invaluable insight into Freud the man and Freud the pioneer of psychoanalysis.

Another important friend during these difficult years was Freud's sister-in-law Minna. She was Martha's younger and not-as-pretty sister who had chosen not to marry when her fiancé had died of tuberculosis. In Minna, Freud found an intelligent woman with whom he could discuss his work. In 1895 Minna became a permanent resident at Berggasse 19. She not only helped Martha with the children but became an important companion for Freud.

Seduction and dreams

Freud's theories about the unconscious mind were a lifetime's work. As a result, it is not possible to give actual dates for his discoveries.

As quickly as Freud established one theory, he discovered something else and revised his ideas. Freud's work took years of defining but he used the word "psychoanalysis" for the first time in 1896. Unlike most great discoveries though, this one went virtually unseen, buried in a paper Freud had published in France.

The Seduction Theory

At this time Freud was voicing another new idea about hysteria that he'd been working through for years. In *Studies in Hysteria* Freud had touched on sexuality, and in the case study of Katharina he even proposed that something in the subject's childhood had caused her neurosis. Now he was developing a theory that all hysteria could be explained by sexual abuse in childhood. Freud concluded that it was repressed memories of seduction by an older person, possibly a relative or servant, that created symptoms in the patient after puberty. He called this the Seduction Theory but when he introduced it in a lecture to the Association for Psychiatry and Neurology on 21 April 1896 it was not well received. Until then most people accepted that hysteria was caused by something physical, perhaps a lesion on the brain, while others believed that nervous conditions were hereditary or imaginary. Freud's claim that he'd found a reason for hysteria that could be cured through therapy should have been exciting. Unfortunately, the mere mention of sexual abuse was too much. One psychiatrist went so far as to call the theory a "scientific fairytale".

Freud was out in the cold – if members of his own profession were appalled, how would ordinary people respond to such radical ideas? Were the general public really expected to believe that something that happened in infancy, possibly at the hands of somebody within the family circle, was responsible for symptoms of hysteria in adulthood? Freud was making suggestions that rocked the very foundations of the most important of all nineteenth-century institutions – the family.

It was a difficult and lonely time for Freud, yet he managed to keep up a professional front. In letters to Fliess he wasn't as self-assured. The criticism hurt and to make matters worse some of his patients were not responding to treatment. In time, even Freud began to question the Seduction Theory.

A death in the family

Freud's ideas continued to evolve but it was events closer to home that got him thinking in another direction. On 23 October 1896 Freud's father Jacob died, probably from cancer, at the age of 81. "The old man's death has moved me very much," he wrote to Fliess soon after Jacob's death, but not even Freud guessed just how much his father's death would affect him.

For one thing, he was now responsible for his mother as well as his family. Although the Freuds were better off, his theories had yet to earn him a substantial income and supporting his large family was a great pressure. The loss of his father also plunged him into greater despair than he'd ever known; deep-seated neuroses that he'd harboured for years suddenly became worse. He developed a terrible travel phobia, which cut short a trip to Rome. He'd always wanted to visit the Italian capital yet when he was within 80 km (50 miles) of getting there he had to turn back. In addition to this phobia, there was also his addiction to cigars.

Freud recognized these problems and made a brave decision; he would tackle them head-on and analyze himself. If his Seduction Theory were true then didn't it stand to reason that he too had suffered from sexual abuse in his childhood? From 1897 Freud began a period of self-analysis and attempted to interpret his own memories. By putting himself on the couch, and adopting the free association method he used with his patients, Freud looked for answers about his own life. Nobody had ever done this before; he was venturing into new territory.

We don't know exactly what Freud discovered about himself and his relationship with his father during this time, but his doubts about the Seduction Theory grew. In September 1897 Freud finally wrote to Fliess: "And now I want to confide in you immediately the great secret that has slowly been dawning on me in the last few months, I no longer believe in my *neurotica* [theory of neuroses]." Freud now grew more interested in the clues about the unconscious that he believed lay in dreams.

Secrets of the mind

Until Freud the serious investigation into dreams was quite limited. Humankind has always attached some kind of importance to dreams, and in ancient civilizations, such as Egypt or Greece, dreams would be interpreted as prophesies or even messages from the gods. The idea of the dream as some kind of vision of the future lived on through the centuries. Those who chose not to believe this theory had much more basic ideas such as dreams being caused by indigestion!

◀ *Freud's father Jacob in old age – a photograph taken shortly before his death.*

In Freud's own words

"The interpretation of dreams is the royal road to a knowledge of the unconscious activities of the mind." *The Interpretation of Dreams*

In the nineteenth century there had been some studies of dreams, including those of Louis Alfred Maury who'd recorded his self-induced dreams. When water was dripped onto his forehead Maury claimed he dreamed of sweating in Italy, and when Eau de Cologne was held under his nose he reported more fantastic dreams based in Egypt. Freud had certainly read about Maury, but he hoped to discover other causes of dreams. Freud's investigations took him on an entirely different path, leading him to call the interpretation of dreams the "royal road" to discovering the unconscious.

The dream of Irma's injection

It had all begun for Freud in the summer of 1895. That year he experienced more vivid dreams than he had ever known before. Then, on 24 July, he had a dream that intrigued him. The dream began with the Freuds accepting guests in a large hall. Among these guests was a young friend of the family, and patient of Freud's, called Irma. In the dream Freud scolded Irma for not listening to him and told her that her symptoms were her own fault. Irma stood firm and claimed that Freud didn't know the extent of her illness. As is the way with dreams, the story became strange and surreal as Freud looked down Irma's throat. Suddenly, a crowd of Freud's professional friends gathered around. Freud discovered that one of the doctors had given Irma an injection with a dirty

A vision of the future?

In the late 1850s the American author Mark Twain had a terrible dream where he saw his brother Henry's corpse lying in a metal coffin in his sister's home. In the dream, a single red flower was placed on his chest. A few weeks later Henry was killed in a riverboat disaster. When Mark Twain came to see the corpse it was laid out in a metal coffin, just as in his dream, but Twain noticed that there was no flower laid on his brother's chest. As he stood looking at the body a woman quietly entered the room. She then laid a bouquet of white flowers with a single red rose gently upon the body.

needle, and this had been the cause of her illness. As with all dreams, "the Dream of Irma's Injection", as it was called in Freud's *The Interpretation of Dreams*, was a jumble of images, but Freud believed that the dream was fulfilling his own wishes. He took the various strands of the dream and traced them back to his own life. He recognized Irma as one of his real-life patients, and the doctor as one of his colleagues who had recently criticized him for not curing this patient. He realized that in his dream he could blame another doctor for Irma's illness. This was reassuring for Freud, who sometimes suffered fainting fits in the company of doctors he found intimidating. It also satisfied his deep-seated need for revenge against the other doctor who had criticized him.

Theories about dreams

Over the next four years Freud continued to study dreams, particularly his own. Some of his interpretations seem far-fetched to us now, but Freud made some important discoveries. He found that when people dreamed they expressed wishes they didn't even know they had. Often these wishes were sexual and so

▲ *The Belle Vue, a resort hotel near Vienna. Freud interpreted his first dream ("Irma's injection") here in the summer of 1895.*

unacceptable that the dreamer had guiltily pushed them to the back of their mind, or repressed them in their unconscious. When a person dreamed, these wishes would re-emerge but they would be so well disguised or hidden in the symbols in the dream that the dreamer didn't recognize them. The work of the doctor was to help the patient unravel these symbols and find their true meaning. Freud believed that dreaming was normal but if somebody had a particular neurosis then their dreams could be interpreted and used to find the cause of their problem.

The Oedipus complex

As Freud immersed himself in self-analysis and interpretation of his own dreams he was often depressed and his nervous symptoms got worse. He likened the experience to looking into a "dung heap", or "grubbing about in human dirt" as he discovered the filthiest and foulest of secrets about himself. By sorting through these dark corners of his mind, Freud found repressed hatred and hidden desires.

An interpretation of a dream

Freud remembered one of his own dreams that he'd had on a train journey from Vienna when there had been no lavatory in his carriage. The dream had ended with Freud on Vienna station, accompanied by an old gentleman. Freud had awoken from the dream just as he had handed the old man a glass urinal. Upon waking, Freud found that he himself needed to urinate.

By remembering an embarrassing incident when he was about seven years old, Freud was able to interpret this dream. He recalled an occasion where he had urinated in his parents' bedroom in their presence. They were angry, and his father said: "The boy will come to nothing!" Freud realized that this reprimand had scarred him because it was a direct blow at his ambition.

Freud deduced that the old man in the dream was his father, and by publicly shaming the old man in the dream Freud was able to fulfil an unconscious wish to have revenge upon his father for the real-life incident. This unconscious wish had been repressed since childhood but had manifested itself in his strange dream.

Perhaps more shocking were the repressed murderous feelings he'd felt towards his father, and the repressed sexual longing he felt for his mother. Freud was tracing complex sexual feelings that went back to his childhood, and he tried applying them to the development of all humans. He believed that when a boy reaches about five years old and starts playing with his penis he becomes sexually interested in his mother. By wishing to gain possession of his mother he becomes hostile towards his father. This hatred is accompanied by a fear that his father will retaliate, possibly by castrating him.

Freud later named this theory after a story by the Greek playwright Sophocles. In this play the central character, Oedipus, unknowingly murders his father then marries his mother. Freud believed that these infant wishes left their mark on the unconscious, so he called his new theory the Oedipus Complex. In the nineteenth century, and even today, ideas like these would not win Freud many followers: he was making suggestions about childhood sexuality that are too shocking to think about. The theory does have some basic

▶ *Oedipus, as portrayed in Sophocles's tragedy, from a French engraving of 1881.*

flaws or omissions, too. How would the Oedipus Complex apply to the development of girls, for example?

▲ Sigmund and Martha Freud (middle row, centre left) and their children with their aunt Minna Bernays (middle row, centre right) at a family birthday party in about 1900. The boys wear fancy party hats.

Penis envy

Freud's version of the female Oedipus Complex was less convincing. Freud believed that girls were also sexually interested in their mother until they discovered they didn't have a penis. Upon this realization the girl would blame her mother for her "inferiority", and turn to her father as a love object instead. As a result she would begin to fantasize that her father would make her pregnant, and that a child from that union would compensate for her not having a penis. The stage of development would be complete when the girl finally realized that other men could make her pregnant, and that having a baby would overcome her feelings of inferiority.

Freud himself placed the Oedipus Complex at the very centre of his theories. Today, after hot debate, psychoanalysts have decided to place less emphasis on the theory, but they do accept that Freud revolutionized the way we think about a child's development, and the great influence this has on how an individual develops into an adult.

Once more Freud's theories were not well received. However, he hoped to better his reputation by applying to the Viennese Ministry of Education to become an unsalaried professor at the University of Vienna. Such a post would be good for his practice, and on the face of it Freud appeared an ideal candidate. In his neat dark suits he looked the part of the conventional professional. Freud was also a workaholic who spent up to eight or nine hours a day with patients and wrote his books long into the night.

However, Freud's revolutionary ideas, and possibly the fact that he was Jewish, meant he was constantly passed over for a professorship. Freud was angry at the ministry's rejection but his work on "the dream book" took over. He became passionate, even obsessive about finishing the book. At one point he even turned to alcohol, of which he didn't approve, to attempt to help his creativity.

The Interpretation of Dreams

In 1900 Freud published *The Interpretation of Dreams*. This work was his masterpiece, combining dream analysis and theories about the unconscious. Although he finished the book in 1899, Freud waited until the new century before unleashing on the world what is now considered to be the first book about psychoanalysis.

At first, the book was heavily criticized in certain quarters and Freud was even called a pornographer. It was not exactly a best-seller, either – in six years the book sold just 300 copies. Nowadays it is recognized as one of the most significant works of the twentieth century.

Freudian slips

By 1900 Freud had transformed his theories about the unconscious into a new science called psychoanalysis. However, he still lived under the shadow of self-doubt and melancholy.

One of Freud's greatest fears was that his work would be dismissed as a "Jewish" science. He also believed that at the age of 44 he was "an old, somewhat shabby Jew" who would certainly die by the time he reached his early sixties. This certainty was rooted in a peculiar theory that had been introduced to him by his friend Fliess. The unconventional ear, nose and throat specialist believed that major changes in life, such as birth and death, moved in cycles. These cycles could be predicted using calculations based on the numbers 23 and 28.

Freud had been convinced by Fliess's weird system and over the years had become increasingly superstitious about numbers. By 1899 Freud believed that the numbers 61 and 62 had appeared in his life so often that they must signify the age he'd be when he died. It seems strange that a man with Freud's intellect could believe in such a system, but Freud was by no means a straightforward man. Even though he was a doctor who wanted to heal the minds of others he suffered from phobias, nervous disorders and obsessive habits of his own. He eventually got over his travel phobia and managed to visit Rome, but he never got over his fainting spells.

He also developed a curious obsession for collecting antique statuettes. In his consulting room at Berggasse 19 he had built up a collection of sculptures that had to be crammed into a cabinet and crowded on to his desk. He could hardly have enjoyed the beauty of each statuette, yet he wrote to Fliess that "the things put me in high spirits and speak of distant times and hands".

Pleasurable pursuits

By 1900 Freud was finally making enough money from his clients to be able to live comfortably. Despite his tendency to overwork he did find time for some relaxation. He enjoyed reading, especially

English literature, and on his heavily laden bookshelves works by Shakespeare stood next to books on psychology and archaeology.

Freud wasn't very interested in music – in fact, he claimed to be tone deaf. He liked certain operas but the Freuds would rarely go to the opera house or the theatre. Other pleasures included playing chess, eating good food and smoking cigars. Each day Martha ensured that a fine three-course lunch was served promptly at 1 p.m. Freud disliked fussy French cooking; his favourite dish was boiled beef and artichokes.

He also seemed unashamed of his smoking. His consulting room was often choked up with cigar smoke and he once told his nephew: "'My boy, smoking is one of the greatest and cheapest enjoyments in life, and if you decide in advance not to smoke, I can only feel sorry for you." Other treats were regular walking holidays when he could enjoy fresh air and nature at its best.

Relationships
It was while he was on holiday in July 1900 that Freud's friendship with Fliess began to go stale. The men had arranged a few days together in the mountains of the Austrian Alps, near Innsbruck. It was while they were walking in the mountains that the two men began quarrelling about psychoanalysis. Years later Fliess claimed that Freud had planned to murder him that day by pushing him off a cliff. This accusation has never been proved but the friendship that had once been so important to Freud was near its end.

A few days later Freud met his wife Martha and sister-in-law Minna in Italy. The threesome set off to enjoy the Italian mountains but after a week Martha grew bored and decided to leave. For two weeks Minna and Freud travelled alone. Some historians suggest that they had an affair during this time, but like so much about Freud's life we will never know.

Making sense of mistakes
When Freud returned from his holidays he began work on *The Psychopathology of Everyday Life*. Unlike *The Interpretation of Dreams* this would be a popular book, perhaps because ordinary things, such as jokes, slips of the tongue, accidents and even forgetfulness were now up for scrutiny. Freud wanted to show that

In Freud's own words

"The psychoanalyst, like the archaeologist in his excavations, must uncover layer after layer of the patient's psyche, before coming to the deepest, most valuable treasures."

everyday mistakes or "parapraxes" were caused by repressed, unconscious thoughts. Like dreams, these slips had a hidden meaning which could be discovered using the free association technique. These days it's common practice for people to call these slips of the tongue or mistakes "Freudian slips" but when Freud made the connection between these everyday instances and the unconscious it was a new idea.

Freud had arrived at his latest theory by interpreting the slips and mistakes of his patients and by delving into his own life. One of his female patients, who had a tendency to boss her sick husband about, had told Freud of a visit to the doctor in which her husband had asked about his diet. The doctor had told the patient's

◀ Minna Bernays, Freud's sister-in-law. Some historians suggest that she and Freud had a romantic affair in 1900 while on holiday.

husband he didn't need a special diet. The woman told Freud: "He can eat and drink what I want." Freud interpreted the use of "I" as opposed to "he" as a slip of the tongue that revealed the woman's repressed emotional urge to dominate her husband. Freud chose examples from his own life too, including the occasion when he kept on forgetting to buy some blotting paper (Löschpapier in German). He then remembered that though he wrote Löschpapier he usually used the other word for blotting paper, Fliesspapier. "Fliess" was obviously the name of his friend, but their relationship was turning sour. Perhaps his forgetfulness could be blamed on Freud's repressed anxiety about the friendship?

The Psychopathology of Everyday Life was eventually published in 1901, although Freud would later add more volumes. Even though the book was a success with the general public as well as scientists, it did have its critics. Some of Freud's examples or case studies seemed exaggerated and far-fetched, while one American medical journal suggested that this new idea could make neurotics even worse because they would try to analyze everything in life.

The curious case of "Dora"

As Freud's work on *The Psychopathology of Everyday Life* came to an end he began writing up the case study of one of his young female patients. Over his career Freud wrote about 133 of his patients, and of these he only wrote about six in any depth. "Dora", whose real name was Ida Bauer, was his first recorded case study and it became the model for psychoanalysis. However, this case revealed as much about Freud as it did about Dora, and it has been the subject of much criticism, especially by feminists, over the years.

Dora was the eighteen-year-old daughter of an unhappily married couple. Her parents had become friendly with another married couple that, in the case study, Freud called Herr and Frau K. From early adolescence, young Dora had been mixed up in a series of events that would trigger hysterical symptoms such as headaches and recurring coughs. To start with her father had taken Frau K as his mistress. Then, when Dora was 16, Herr K had made unwelcome sexual advances towards her. Dora had always trusted and admired Herr K but she now claimed she hated him. Dora's father took Herr K's

Feminists respond

"Freud never showed much concern with the destiny of woman; it is clear that he simply adapted his account from that of the destiny of man, with slight modifications."
Simone de Beauvoir, 1949

"Freud is the father of psychoanalysis. It had no mother."
Germaine Greer, 1970

side, believing him to be innocent over his daughter, who he thought was having fantasies. Soon after, Dora's symptoms grew worse and she declined into depression, threatening to commit suicide. She started seeing Freud in October 1900, but after 11 weeks she called a halt to the treatment. Freud was angry and disappointed because he believed he was about to cure her.

Nevertheless, the case had been a turning point for him because he believed that he had used dream interpretation successfully and that the case demonstrated his Oedipal Complex to perfection. Later, Freud was criticized because he seemed to mould his interpretation to make it fit perfectly. He had decided early on that Dora had fallen in love with Herr K. Even when Dora vehemently denied she was in love with Herr K, Freud said that she was saying "no" when she really meant "yes". The truth seemed to be that Freud had bullied his patient into saying what he believed she meant.

Transference

The case did not end there. In 1902 Dora returned to Freud's treatment rooms. By this time Freud had observed something else about his female patients. In the course of their treatment, some women came to feel a romantic attachment to him, and on one occasion a patient had even kissed him full on the mouth. Freud could easily have believed these women had fallen in love with him, but he didn't see it that way. He believed his patients were transferring their passionate feelings for someone else in their life, usually a parent, on to him.

When Dora came back to see him in 1902 Freud began fully to understand this phenonemon. He realized that Dora had transferred her unconscious feelings for her father on to him. When she cut short the treatment she had been exacting her revenge on her father. Freud was annoyed because he hadn't been able to recognize "transference" when he first treated Dora. From this time on he looked out for "transference" and used it to help other patients to understand the root of their illnesses.

e father of psychoanalysis"

The year 1902 would be a good one for Freud. His work was finally being recognized and, at long last, he was appointed a professor at the University of Vienna.

In March of that year Freud wrote a letter to Fliess about the professorship but his tone was more sarcastic than celebratory and, as always, work came first: "Congratulations and flowers are already pouring in, as though the role of sexuality has suddenly been officially recognized by His Majesty," he wrote. "I myself would still gladly exchange every five congratulations for one decent case suitable for extensive treatment."

The Wednesday group

Freud began to host small gatherings of practitioners at his rooms each Wednesday evening after supper to discuss psychoanalysis. The group, composed entirely of Jewish physicians, would become known as the Wednesday Psychological Society. The meetings were the idea of a young nerve doctor and part-time journalist, Wilhelm Stekel. Stekel was impressed by Freud, and had written a glowing newspaper review of *The Interpretation of Dreams*. On the strength of Freud's work, Stekel was now considering a career in psychoanalysis too. Freud liked the idea of regular meetings and invited Stekel, together with Max Rahane, Rudolf Reitler and Alfred Adler to Berggasse 19.

At the first gathering they discussed the significance of smoking cigars – a subject so close to Freud's heart. In later sessions they talked about things that might seem mundane, such as doodling, but the men picked over the subject and found that even mindless drawings could reveal unconscious wishes. With the flow of black coffee and cake, and the clouds of cigar smoke billowing out of the room, it was sometimes difficult to remember that these men were discussing something

The University of Vienna, as photographed in 1890. Freud was appointed professor there in 1902.

serious. The debates could be lively and most enjoyable, as were the feelings of comradeship and exhilaration at discussing a new branch of science with like-minded colleagues. Freud was very much the leader of the group, and although he was open to the younger men's ideas he didn't like it if they disagreed with him.

It was to be an inspiring time for everybody, including Freud, and for the first time he was not alone with his theories. For many years Fliess had provided Freud with the support and respect that he obviously needed, but now he had a band of disciples around him.

Essays on sexuality

As well as his Wednesday meetings Freud gave lectures each Saturday at Vienna's General Hospital. By now he had gained some credibility within scientific circles

▲ *The courtyard of the Vienna General Hospital, where Freud delivered Saturday lectures.*

but the number of people attending his lectures rarely hit double figures. It seemed that the new century hadn't changed people's minds about sexuality. The masses were simply not ready yet for Freud's theories. Freud battled on, and by 1904 he had published *Three Essays on Sexuality* which pulled together his

theories so far about the sexual origins of neurosis. Freud's main interest was in why people became neurotic, but as a scientist he had to look at different forms of human behaviour. He began his work by looking at why some people were attracted to people of the same sex, or why other people had certain sexual perversions. Once again he suggested that it was because of something that had happened in childhood. He then introduced the idea that neurosis was caused because the child's sexual development had been interrupted, or gone wrong, at a particular time. Freud believed that each person was born with a basic sex drive that he named the *libido*. He said that the libido was an emotional energy that underlay all conscious and unconscious drives. Freud went on to suggest that newborn babies were born with an unstructured libido. Therefore they took pleasure from stimulation of any part of their body, but from an early age developed different pleasure zones.

Childhood development

Freud said there were distinct stages of sexual development and these related to different parts or zones of the body. He believed that in the first year of a child's life, libido was centred on food and the mouth and the pleasure they derived from sucking at their mother's breast or sucking their thumb – for this reason he called the first zone the oral stage. Between the ages of one and three Freud believed the child moved on to the second zone, the anal stage. This was when they learned how to control their own bowels, and derived great pleasure from their ability to "hold on" or "let go". The third zone of a child's development Freud called the phallic stage. He said that this happened at about the age of three or four when a child began playing with its own genitals and discovered that this action could be a source of pleasure. The final stage of development was not reached until after puberty at which time a person would be able to achieve sexual pleasure with another person.

Freud believed that neuroses in adult life came about because one of the earlier stages had gone wrong. The book *Three Essays on Sexuality* was one of Freud's most important works, but the world still wasn't ready for Freud's shocking theories. In those days sex most certainly did not sell, and the 1,000 copies printed in 1904 took four years to sell out.

A code of practice

By 1904 Freud was also defining what he considered to be the best way of practising psychoanalysis. Freud was adamant that new patients should be chosen with care, and in some ways he sounded like a snob: "If the physician has to deal with a worthless character, he soon loses the interest which makes it possible for him to enter profoundly into the patient's mental life." He also felt his patients should be reasonably well-educated and wealthy.

These stipulations also had a practical purpose. Psychoanalysis sessions were not cheap, and Freud was recommending six months to three years of treatment. He also urged his patients to attend sessions up to six times a week. Freud's other suggestions included how a treatment room should be organized. His own patients reclined on the couch, a practice he started in 1892 when he adopted the free association method. Freud used a couch throughout his career because he believed it encouraged the patient to talk.

Freud also believed that the psychoanalyst should sit out of the patient's view, where they wouldn't be swayed by the changing facial expressions of their analyst. Again, there was a practical side to this arrangement. Freud often saw patients for up to eight hours a day, and the thought of being face-to-face with other people for so long was rather off-putting. Freud made other suggestions such as listening to the patients rather than taking notes. He thought it best for a psychoanalyst to keep some kind of professional distance from their patient: "I cannot advise my colleagues too urgently to model themselves during psychoanalytic treatment on the surgeon, who puts aside all his feelings, even his human sympathy, and concentrates his mental forces on the single aim of performing the operation as skilfully as possible."

As with his psychoanalytic theories, Freud would often go back and redefine the techniques he felt worked in psychoanalysis. In later years he recommended that psychoanalysts should only treat people they had never met before. It was a rule that he would break himself years later when he analyzed his youngest daughter, Anna.

The father figure

In 1905 Anna Freud was ten years old and surrounded by teenage brothers and sisters. With long working hours and dedication to his science it was a wonder that Freud had time for his six children, but he was a caring and conscientious

parent. In his early letters to Fliess he often wrote about his children with love and obvious pleasure. He described his daughter Sophie as his "ray of sunshine" and "the most beautiful thing". He even quoted bits of poetry written by his eight-year-old son Martin.

Over the years the health of his children brought him many worries. In 1905 his daughter Mathilde nearly died from appendicitis. On hearing she would survive Freud threw one of his slippers at one of his beloved ancient statuettes and watched it break into pieces.

Martin, Freud's eldest son, recalled that their childhood was different compared to other children's lives at the time: "We were never ordered to do this or not to do that," he remembered. "We were never told not to ask questions. Replies and explanations to all sensible questions were always given by our parents, who treated us as individuals, persons in our own right."

Though Freud adopted what seems a modern approach towards parenting, in many other ways he was a product of his time. As father, he was head of the household and expected his children to be well behaved and respectful. At times he could be rather formal and he rarely hugged or kissed any of his children. One of his express wishes for all his children was that none of them should follow him into the science of psychoanalysis.

Visitors from abroad

In 1906 the Wednesday Psychological Society had 17 members. Freud had great respect for some of these early members, particularly Otto Rank, Paul Federn and Eduard Hitschmann, but he was aware that the initial enthusiasm and comradeship had waned. The group needed new blood, especially from abroad. Between 1906 and 1908 the Wednesday Society played host to many overseas visitors who were curious to know more of Dr Freud and his work. In 1907 the Swiss practitioners Max Eitingon, Carl Gustav Jung, Ludwig Binswanger and Karl Abraham came to Berggasse 19. In the following year Abraham Brill from the USA, Ernest Jones from the UK and Edoardo Weiss from Italy paid a visit. Freud was happy to introduce these men to his circle, and he hoped that they would take psychoanalysis back to their own countries.

Part of a letter from Freud to Jung

"... Whether you have been or will be lucky or unlucky, I do not know; but now of all times I wish I were with you, taking pleasure in no longer being alone and, if you are in need of encouragement, telling you about my long years of honourable but painful solitude, which began after I cast my first glance into the new world, about the indifference and incomprehension of my closest friends, about the terrifying moments when I myself thought I had gone astray and was wondering how I might still make my misled life useful to my family, about my slowly growing conviction, which fastened itself to the interpretation of dreams as a rock in a stormy sea..."
2 September 1907

Carl Gustav Jung

In 1907 Freud's hopes for the future of psychoanalysis rested to a large extent on the work of the Swiss psychiatrist Carl Gustav Jung (1875-1961). Jung was a psychiatrist working at a mental institute in Burghölzli in Zürich, and had been the first practitioner outside Vienna to show an interest in the work of Freud. Although Jung had read *The Interpretation of Dreams*

A 1904 portrait of the Swiss psychiatrist Carl G Jung.

he used his own techniques to treat patients with psychotic illnesses. He later found that the word-association tests he had devised worked well with Freud's free association technique. Jung wrote a paper about his findings and sent a copy to Freud in 1906. Freud promptly wrote back congratulating the young psychiatrist, and so began a correspondence and collaboration that would be as close and warm as Freud had experienced with Fliess. To start with their letters were professional but in time they became more intimate and spoke of family matters too.

The two men met for the first time on 3 March 1907, but Freud had already been addressing Jung as "Dear Friend" in their letters. Over the following years their relationship became more like that of father and son. Though Jung initially disagreed with some of Freud's sexual theories he was happy to work alongside the man he worshipped. Freud, for his part, was happy to find somebody he believed was worthy of inheriting the leadership of the psychoanalytic movement.

International fame

In April 1908 the Wednesday Society changed its name to the Vienna Psychoanalytic Society.

That same month the first International Congress of Psychology and Neurology was held at the Hotel Bristol in Salzburg. It wasn't a large congress because all those attending had to fund their own trip, but the "friends of psychoanalysis" came from far and wide, including Vienna, Zurich, Berlin, Budapest, London and New York.

Papers were given by Sigmund Freud, Carl Jung, Alfred Adler, Sandor Ferenczi, Karl Abraham and Ernest Jones. All these men played a part in the history of psychoanalysis. At that time, however, they were considered loners in a branch of science that many still felt was dubious because of its sexual connections.

Freud's paper was the highlight of the congress. Until now he hadn't given much away about his techniques. This was because he was still learning himself, and because he liked to keep some of his methods a secret. When Freud spoke at Salzburg he gave a tantalizing glimpse of how he worked, as well as a talk about one of his latest cases, that of a 29-year-old lawyer called Ernst Lanzer. In time Freud would write about this famous case study and name his patient the Rat Man.

The Rat Man

Ernst Lanzer had first come to Freud in October 1907. He was a likeable young man who in their first hour together told Freud lots of amusing stories. It would have been hard to imagine that such an apparently "normal" person was living under a shadow, but Lanzer was doing just that. For a long time he had been plagued by a terrible fear that something awful would happen to the people he most cared for, particularly his father and his close female friend. This fear was centred on an Eastern punishment that he had heard about while he was in the army. The punishment involved tying a pot of rats onto a criminal's buttocks so that they could eat their way into the body. When Lanzer tried to tell Freud about this he became extremely agitated, and lashed out at Freud. Eventually Lanzer managed to explain that he

feared this punishment would be enacted on his female friend. As a result of his fear, Lanzer had begun carrying out various obsessive rituals, such as paying bills that had already been paid, in the hope that he could prevent the dreadful event from really happening.

Lanzer received treatment for about a year, at which point Freud declared his patient was cured. At Salzburg Freud could only introduce the case as it was still ongoing, but he was able to give his audience a real-life example of how his theories worked. With Lanzer he was able to show that it was problems in early childhood, and in this case the love-hate relationship with a father, that had caused his patient to develop an obsessive-compulsive disorder. When

▲ *Vienna in the early 1900s. As Freud's reputation grew, many patients made special trips to his consulting room at Berggasse 19.*

Freud left the congress at Salzburg he felt refreshed and optimistic about the future. The truth about psychoanalysis was finally being heard.

Little Hans

Another case that was important to Freud came his way that summer. Freud believed that it was more effective to treat younger people. In fact, he went so far as to suggest that patients over 50 years old were beyond help. In the case of "Little Hans" Freud had the opportunity to try his technique on a five-year-old child. "Hans" was actually Herbert Graf, the son of Max Graf, an early member of the Wednesday Society. The Grafs' interest in psychoanalysis had prompted them to follow Freud's example of child-rearing, and Herbert had rarely been scolded by his liberal parents.

Herbert had developed into a loving and bright child but in January 1908 he suddenly developed a phobia that a horse would bite him. The fear grew so real that Herbert began avoiding places where he might see horses. Herbert's father reported these strange symptoms to Freud but it wasn't until the summer, when Herbert's baby sister was born, that the phobia became so bad that he could hardly leave the house for fear of horses. It was at this point that Freud began treating the frightened child.

As with all cases the art of listening carefully to the patient was vital, and Freud soon realized that Herbert was the perfect little Oedipus, who had developed an unconscious fear of his father. Apparently, Herbert had been caught masturbating by his mother when he was very young. The Grafs were liberal but the act of masturbation was considered so bad in those days that they had told their son off for his inappropriate behaviour. This scolding had made such a deep impression on Herbert that he developed a castration complex. At the same time Herbert had noticed the genitalia of male horses, and had identified their large penises with that of his father. Freud deduced that Herbert's fear of his father was displaced on to horses. Once Freud had interpreted Herbert's symptoms he was able to reassure Herbert that one day he would be as big as his father. In time, Herbert overcame his phobia of horses.

Freud was delighted with the case of Little Hans because it fitted his theories so well. In the past, particularly in Dora's case, people had suggested that Freud had forced his theories to fit the situation, but with Hans he'd found the embodiment of his childhood sexuality theory.

Across the Atlantic

Freud's work was still considered highly controversial, yet in 1909 he received an invitation that gave him great encouragement. The president of Clark University in Worcester, Massachusetts, USA had written to inform Freud that the university had awarded him an honorary degree. He invited Freud to visit Clark to collect the award. Freud had mixed feelings about the United States but he had to admit that

Americans seemed to take a serious interest in psychology. This interest was evident in the number of people setting up practices, and the formation of the "Boston School" of psychotherapy. It was also evident in the number of articles about psychology that circulated in the popular press. In Europe psychoanalysis was still viewed with suspicion and the media kept clear of the subject. Freud realized that a visit to the USA could be a good thing for the future of psychoanalysis.

On 20 August he set sail with his companions, Jung and Ferenczi. In those days it took eight days to cross the Atlantic, but during the long hours at sea the three men enjoyed analyzing each other's dreams. By now Freud had interpreted some of the disguised images commonly found in dreams. Objects that suggested receptacles, such as boxes, houses or caves, came to symbolize the vagina. Objects that suggested penetration, like snakes, swords or guns, represented the penis.

Once the men had arrived in the USA they headed for New York. There they met the psychiatrists Ernest Jones and Abraham Brill who showed them the sights of this exciting city. A week later, on 10 September, they attended the ceremony at Clark University. In his opening speech Freud thanked Clark for giving "the first official recognition of our endeavours". Over the next week Freud gave five lectures, delivering his papers to some of America's leading professors and psychologists. In the first of his lectures he paid a generous tribute to Breuer by claiming that Breuer had been the founder of psychoanalysis.

Though some people found Freud's theories shocking, he was well received. He remained critical of the USA – he complained about the food and he hated it when somebody slapped him on the back and said, "Hi, Doc!" In general, though, he was pleased that he was treated with respect: "In Europe I felt as though I were despised," he later wrote about his visit, "but over there I found myself received by the foremost men as an equal. As I stepped on to the platform at Worcester … it seemed like the realization of some incredible day-dream."

▶ *A portrait of Freud taken in 1909, the year he travelled to the USA to collect an honorary degree.*

An international movement

The trip to the USA marked a turning point. However, just as the psychoanalysis movement was picking up momentum abroad, there were problems at home. Arguments within the Vienna Psychoanalytic Society seemed to reach boiling point, particularly with Stekel and Adler, and Freud became increasingly disillusioned with the Viennese members.

At the age of 54, Freud was beginning to feel tired and weary, and he hoped that he could pass the responsibility of the movement to his young protégé, the man he called the "crown prince", Carl Jung. His plans for the future included a new international group, with Jung as its president. In 1910 at the Second International Psychoanalytical Congress held at the Grand Hotel in Nuremberg, Ferenczi presented proposals for the establishment of The International Psychoanalytical Association (IPA). Freud was excited with this new development and in a letter to Ferenczi said: "The childhood of our movement has ended. That is my impression. I hope it will be followed by a rich and fair time of youth."

Part of a letter from Jung to Freud

"Dear Professor Freud,
I thank you with all my heart for this token of your confidence. The undeserved gift of your friendship is one of the high points in my life which I cannot celebrate with big words. The reference to Fliess – surely not accidental – and your relationship with him impels me to ask you to let me enjoy your friendship not as one between equals but as that of father and son. This distance appears to me fitting and natural. Moreover it alone, so it seems to me, strikes a note that would prevent misunderstandings and enable two hard-headed people to exist alongside one another in an easy and unstrained relationship."
20 February 1908

In time Freud's hopes were dashed. His shameless favouritism towards Jung antagonized the Viennese doctors. Freud tried to pave the way to reconciliation by proposing Adler as the president of the Vienna Society but it was too late. Adler felt too much resentment and refused the post. The matter was made worse because Adler had begun to disagree with Freud on points of theory. He believed that it was a struggle for power in relationships during childhood rather than problems with sexuality that caused hysteria. He also believed there were other ways, rather than free association, to tackle the problem.

Adler and Stekel finally broke away from the movement in 1911 to form the Society for Free Psychoanalytic Investigation. They were the first of Freud's early disciples to go their own way. Inevitably, Freud was drawn closer to Jung. Their relationship seemed sustainable because Freud concentrated upon neurosis, while Jung researched and treated more serious mental illnesses, such as schizophrenia.

Times of conflict and change

The father-son relationship between Jung and Freud was too intense to last; in time their story became an Oedipal drama of its very own.

At the start of their friendship Jung had expressed some reservations about Freud's emphasis on the sexual origins of neurosis, but it wasn't until after their trip to the USA in 1909 that cracks began to appear in their relationship. Just before they had boarded the ship Freud had fainted while in Jung's company. Freud later suggested he was responding to the "murderous wishes" of a son – Freud obviously wasn't as confident as he might appear.

In the meantime Jung was developing his own views about the unconscious. He'd become fascinated by religion and myth, and their effects upon the "collective unconscious". He started writing about his new theory in a book called *Transformations and Symbols of the Libido*. Although Jung was researching a new area, Freud was not

overly concerned. In 1911 he had been working on *Totem and Taboo*, a title that traced the Oedipus Complex back to primitive man, and he mistakenly believed that he and Jung were investigating the same thing. In truth, Jung was taking a new path that would eventually lead him to openly question Freud's theory of childhood sexuality. Inevitably, Freud was hurt by this.

On 24 November 1912 Jung and Freud met at the Park Hotel in Munich. While they were there Freud suffered another fainting spell in front of Jung. As he came round from his stupor he was reported as saying: "How sweet dying must be." Years later Jung wrote that "he [Freud] looked at me as if I were his father." The Oedipal drama

▶ *Freud (circled, left) and Jung (circled, right) appear together at the Weimar Congress in 1911.*

was unfolding before their eyes, but within two months it would be over. Following their stay in Munich Jung wrote to Freud asking him to put aside their professional differences and to remain friends. Unfortunately, by the end of 1912 their letters had become openly critical. Jung complained that Freud tried to psychoanalyze him. He blamed Freud for Adler and Stekel's split from the movement, suggesting that Freud had adopted the role of a father who looked for weaknesses in his "sons". On a more damning note he suggested that Freud should confront his own neuroses. In January 1913 Freud ceased contact with Jung and by 1914 their seven-year friendship was at an end.

The secret council

With Adler, Stekel and Jung each gone their separate ways, Freud might well have felt isolated. However, in the summer of 1912 Ferenczi had suggested that they form a secret inner circle of men who would represent and remain loyal to Freud's theories. Freud had been rather taken with this idea, and called the group "the secret council".

It was his suggestion that they would remain secret at all costs. The members would be Ernest Jones, Sandor Ferenczi, Karl Abraham, Otto Rank and a newcomer, the lawyer Hanns Sachs.

After the Jung debacle, Freud became more defensive about his friendships. In his 1925 autobiography, Freud defended himself against accusations by some that he had a need to turn his friends into enemies. He pointed out that he had remained close to a number of colleagues and he managed to reel off many names besides those in the secret council. Surrounded by his followers, Freud was able to move on from the split with Jung.

Meanwhile Jung worked alone on theories that seemed less accessible than those of his old Viennese mentor but would, in time, become just as important.

Life at home

As Freud's fame was spreading in the outside world, his children were growing up and becoming independent. By 1913 Mathilde and Sophie were married. Ernst and Oliver were studying in Germany and only came home for the holidays. Martin was studying business and law at university. This only left the Freud's youngest child, Anna, at home. She was just 17 and devoted to her father.

Freud always seemed to favour his middle daughter, Sophie, but his special nickname for Anna was *Schwarzer Teufel* (Black Devil). As a child Freud had always enjoyed Anna's mischievous ways, but as she got older he sometimes found his youngest daughter a "little odd". From the age of 13, Anna had shown an interest in psychoanalysis and often sat in the corner listening to the meetings of the Vienna society.

Freud had always told his children not to follow in his footsteps, but in time his mind changed and he encouraged Anna. In early 1914 Freud wrote to his colleague Karl Abraham: "We are no longer a family, only three old people [Freud, Martha and Minna] … Even my little daughter wants to go to England by herself this year." It was while Anna was away in England that World War One began.

World War One

This war, also known as the Great War, would change life for everybody in Europe. Every family had a father, a son or other relative who was called up to fight for their country. The Freuds' sons, Ernst, Oliver and Martin, all fought for Austria.

At the start of the war Freud supported the Austro-German alliance but as casualties increased he became cynical and turned to pacifism. He worried for his sons, and reported dark dreams in which they died. He was also terrified by humankind's potential for aggression. "Our civilization has been disfigured by a gigantic hypocrisy," he wrote. "Can we ever again say we are civilized?"

War brought other hardships such as shortages of food and coal. Patients and friends were kind and gave Freud gifts of food and precious cigars. Even so, he lost weight and shivered in his unheated study. The spread of psychoanalysis was also stalled by the war. Freud attempted to write to his colleagues overseas but many of his letters were censored.

Meanwhile, the number of patients

▲ A 1916 portrait of Freud taken with his sons Ernst (left) and Martin (right, behind) in army uniform.

Ernst, Martin and their brother Oliver all fought with the Austro-Hungarian army during World War One.

dwindled, so Freud turned to writing and giving lectures instead.

In 1916, Freud turned 60 and his letters to his friend Karl Abraham became filled with despair. Freud felt old and tired and believed that he would probably die soon.

There were also some good times however, and in the summers of 1917 and 1918 the Freuds took a holiday in Slovakia. There was also a rumour that Freud might win a Nobel Prize.

The Wolf Man

During the war years Freud continued to define the unconscious, and he would return once more to childhood sexuality in the book *The History of an Infantile Neurosis*, which he began towards the end of 1914. An important part of this new work was the case of a rich young Russian called Serge Pankejeff whom Freud called the "Wolf Man". Pankejeff had first approached Freud in 1910 because of his recurrent attacks of depression and his various symptoms that included a fear of wolves, a compulsion for womanizing and chronic constipation. Freud's analysis eventually centred on Pankejeff's childhood nightmare in which he saw six or seven white wolves sitting in a walnut tree outside his bedroom staring at him. Freud deduced that Pankejeff had seen his parents making love when he was aged about one. Freud had always maintained that witnessing parental intercourse had a traumatic effect on children. He suggested that the white wolves in the dream were in fact representing Pankejeff's parents, dressed in underclothes, and laying on white sheets.

In the past Freud had been accused of making the symptoms of his patients fit his theory, and he may well have done the same again in this case of the wolf man. Even though Freud's interpretations seemed far-fetched, and Pankejeff never remembered seeing his parents having intercourse, this would become one of Freud's most famous cases.

By 1914 Freud had become fond of his young patient and was happy to believe him cured. The story didn't end there though, and after World War One Pankejeff returned to Freud for more treatment. Once again Freud believed

he'd cured his patient but Pankejeff suffered from depression and difficulties in his relationships with women for the rest of his long life. Freud thought the Wolf Man was the best advertisement for his treatment so far, but later psychoanalysts criticized the case and pointed out that Freud had never really cured his patient.

The end of the war

When the war finally ended in November 1918 Freud had completed another paper called *Mourning and Melancholia*. The long war had frightened Freud, and the main theme of this bleak work was death and psychotic depression. His ideas were taking other new directions too. He had once said that he would never analyze somebody he knew, but in October 1918 he began analyzing his own daughter, Anna.

The war also brought unwelcome changes. Inflation meant that the Austrian mark was nearly worthless and Freud had lost the equivalent of

£200,000 in today's money. For the first time when his sons, and some of his sisters, turned to him for financial support Freud couldn't help them. He felt inadequate and was forced to accept money from his brother-in-law Eli Bernays who lived in New York.

Freud had survived the war, but he had aged badly to become a frailer, less optimistic man.

◄ *German troops in action in France during the offensive of June 1918. Freud was deeply disturbed by the events of World War One.*

Mind over matter

In December 1919 the Freuds celebrated their first family Christmas since before the war.

Everybody was present except for Sophie, and although Martha coughed and spluttered and Minna was ill with pleurisy, the family were in fine form. The happiness was to be short-lived, however. In January 1920 Sophie died suddenly from a bout of influenza. Freud was overcome with shock and sorrow: "I do not know whether cheerfulness will ever call on us again," he wrote to a friend, "my poor wife has been hit too hard." Freud took to wearing a photo of Sophie in a locket attached to his watch chain.

Though he hadn't fully recovered from her death he plunged back into work. Keeping himself busy helped him to hang on to his sanity. However, his next book, *Beyond the Pleasure Principle*, published later that year, was his darkest work yet. Freud had already said that human behaviour was motivated by the life instinct, such as the need to find food or to have sex. Now, he believed there was more to the mind and introduced the death instinct. He believed that there was part of us that needed to be satisfied and at peace, in other words, dead. It was a strange idea but he reasoned that our need to "escape" into a book or sleep were all part of the death instinct. Self-destructive behaviour was a more serious version of the death instinct, while aggressive behaviour, and even murder, were the result of the death instinct turned on others.

Ego, id and super-ego

In 1921 Freud published *Group Psychology and the Analysis of the Ego*, and then in 1923 he released *The Ego and the Id*. Once more he revised his psychoanalytic theory, but perhaps the most important discovery of this time was his new model of the mind or psyche. He said that the mind consisted of three parts – the *ego*, *id* and *super-ego*. Today people often say things like somebody has a "large ego" or someone is "on an ego-trip". We mean that that person indulges their own interests or devotes themself to self-expression. When Freud spoke about the ego he meant the conscious part of our mind that guides us in reality – the part of our mind where all conscious perceptions belong, such as reason or common sense.

With the id (Latin for "it") Freud was talking about the unconscious part of the mind that drives people's desires or instincts. It was a primitive, unorganized part of the psyche that Freud described as "the dark, inaccessible part of our personality".

The super-ego was a bit like another part of the ego that judged and often restrained the unconscious drives of the id – in other words it was like unconscious guilt. With some of his patients, Freud had noticed a tendency to get worse before they got better. The patient expressed no guilt openly but Freud believed they had unconscious guilt and desire for punishment that was present in the super-ego.

Freud's model of the ego, id and super-ego helped to explain why people are so complex and act in contradictory ways. It was another revolutionary idea that would change the way people thought about the mind. Like all of Freud's theories, though, it did have its critics, including Freud himself, who over the years would return to his model of the psyche and attempt to re-define the theory.

The spread of psychoanalysis

After the war, and for the rest of his life, Freud's patients would often be people who wanted to practise psychoanalysis. In order to learn how to analyze somebody else they had to be analyzed themselves, and who better to be taught by than the "father of psychoanalysis" himself.

Freud was happy to adapt to this new role because he needed the money, and also because it guaranteed that the science of psychoanalysis would spread. In these years he analyzed many Americans, as well as important followers and apprentices like Dr Jeanne Lampl-de Groot, who later became an important psychoanalyst in Amsterdam, and Princess Marie Bonaparte, the great-granddaughter of Napoleon's brother who worked towards organizing the French psychoanalytic movement.

By the 1920s even a weary and rather

pessimistic Freud had to admit that his new science was finally being accepted in every corner of the world. The Institute of Psychoanalysis in Berlin in Germany became the centre of psychoanalysis in Europe, but there were also thriving institutes in London, Vienna and Budapest, as well as in Holland and Switzerland. By the 1930s there were new groups in Paris, Calcutta and Jerusalem, and in Japan and Scandinavia. Meanwhile psychoanalysis had caught on in the USA, independently of Europe. There were institutes in New York and Chicago, and the USA had the highest number of practising analysts of anywhere else in the world.

Popular culture

The Great War had changed many people's attitude to life, and particularly towards gender and sex. Though some people, often speaking from a religious or medical high-ground, still rejected Freud's theories, these were more lenient times.

Psychoanalysis slowly captured people's imaginations as it became the subject of literature and art. It was also discussed more freely by the media. By the 1920s Freud had become a household name.

Terms coined by him, such as the Oedipus Complex or the ego and the id now became part of fashionable people's vocabularies. Freud had been offered large sums of money by a US newspaper to analyze two notorious murderers. The movie producer Sam Goldwyn even asked Freud to act as script consultant on one of his blockbuster movies.

Freud turned down such offers as he wanted to safeguard the serious image of psychoanalysis. He wasn't keen on being famous either: "In England and America there is now a great … ballyhoo, which however, I don't like and which brings me nothing but newspaper clippings and visits from interviewers. Still, though, it is amusing."

Illness and despair

Ill health was another reason why Freud did not court the limelight. In 1923 a mouth ulcer that refused to go away was diagnosed as cancer of the jaw. Years of smoking more than twenty cigars a day had finally caught up with him. Freud went through a series of harrowing and

▶ *Despite being diagnosed with cancer of the jaw in 1923, Freud refused to give up smoking cigars. This portrait dates from 1926.*

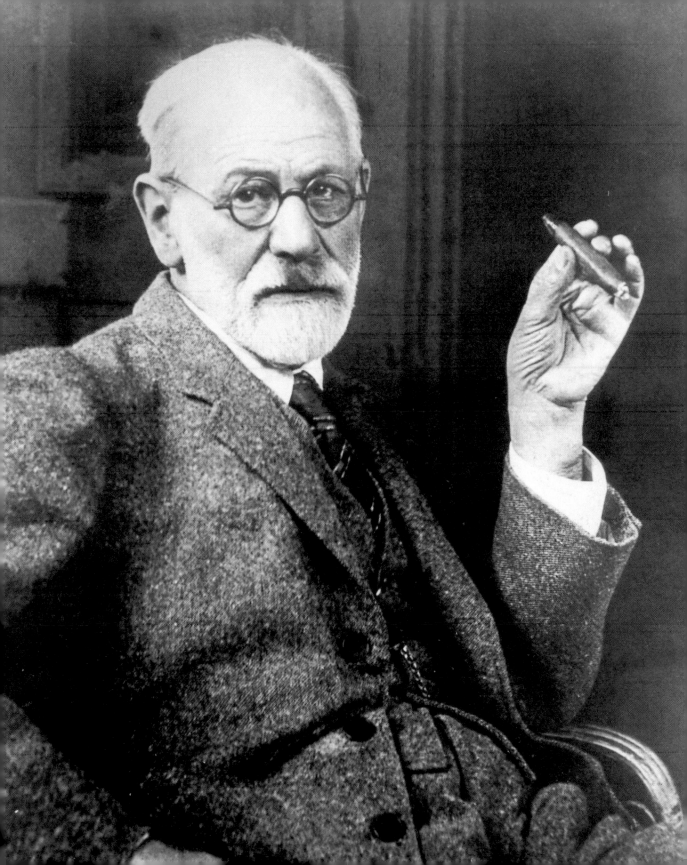

painful operations – the first operation was almost the last as Freud nearly bled to death. Over the years he endured 33 different operations on his jaw and had to wear a prosthesis, a kind of giant pair of dentures, that he would nickname "the monster". This cumbersome device kept his oral and nasal cavities separate but it was painful to wear and had to be kept scrupulously clean. It made eating and talking very difficult, but Freud refused to give up smoking. Sometimes he even used a peg to hold the prosthesis in place so he could get enough suction on his cigar. Freud trained himself to speak again but his illness meant that he never ate in public, or gave lectures again.

While Freud battled against cancer there was tragedy and betrayal to contend with, too. In June 1923 his four-year-old grandson, Heinele, died from tuberculosis. He was the son of his beloved daughter, Sophie, and Freud had displaced his love of his daughter onto her child. When Heinele died Freud did something he rarely did: he cried. It was a dreadful time: "I am still being tormented by my snout," he told a friend, "and obsessed by impotent longing for the dear child."

Freud's depression deepened when his long-time colleague Otto Rank wrote a book that questioned Freud's techniques. Rank now believed that it was trauma at birth that caused neurosis. He thought that long drawn-out sessions where the patients sifted through memories were unnecessary. Instead, he proposed just a few months of therapy.

Yet, throughout these turbulent times, Freud still found comfort in his work. By early 1924 the flow of patients at Berggasse 19 had picked up again and Freud was writing *An Autobiographical Study*.

The dutiful daughter

Through these dark years Freud also came to rely upon his daughter Anna. She was the only one of his children who hadn't married, and in the final years of his life she became his companion, his colleague and his nurse. Anna had always adored her father, and many people suggest that this is why she hadn't married.

Theirs was an unusual relationship, made more so because Freud had started analyzing Anna in 1918. "She has an extraordinary gift for being unhappy," Freud once said of his youngest daughter.

▶ *A relaxed 1929 photograph of Freud at breakfast with Martha (left) and Minna (centre).*

He continued to treat her on and off until 1924. In that year Anna began to take patients of her own, and in time became a child psychoanalyst. At this time, it was still rare for a woman to be involved in science. It is a mark of Freud's respect for his daughter that he educated her to become his successor.

A sick old man

When Otto Rank left the Secret Council Freud had been disappointed but in 1926 he lost his friend Karl Abraham to lung cancer. The death of his colleague at just 48 was a terrible blow to Freud, who himself turned 70 not long afterwards.

By now he was not in good health but he continued to see patients and even began to write on new topics. In 1927 he wrote about religion in *The Future of an Illusion*. Even though he was Jewish by birth he had been an atheist since his school days. Now in old age he returned to a subject that had always fascinated him. Predictably, he criticized religion and went so far as to suggest that too much religion was bad for people. At a time when religion was still important to society his views were shocking to many.

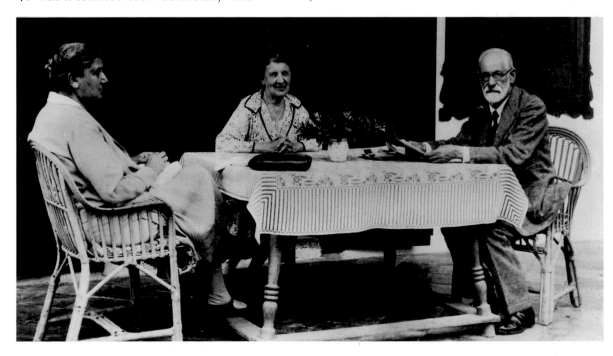

To die in freedom

As Freud got older he became even more pessimistic. In 1930 he published *Civilization and its Discontents*, a book he had considered calling *Unhappiness in Culture*.

This time Freud suggested that though humans were driven to seek pleasure, they actually spent more effort avoiding pain. He said: "the intention that man should be 'happy' is not contained in the plan of 'Creation'." Freud wasn't sure about his new book, but it would go on to become one of his most influential works. In August 1930 he was also awarded the Goethe Prize for Literature. For many years Freud had been passed over for a Nobel Prize, so it was a great honour. Unfortunately he was too weak to travel to Germany to collect the prize.

Rumours of his ill health began to circulate but when death visited the Freud family in September of that year it was his 95-year-old mother who passed away. Freud knew that the death of a mother was one of the hardest things a person would go through but in some ways he felt relieved, "since it was always an abhorrent thought that she would learn of my death, and secondly the satisfaction that she has at last the deliverance to which she had acquired the right in so long a life." Perhaps with his mother dead, Freud felt that he could die in peace but when he caught pneumonia that October he managed to fight the illness. The will to live had obviously not abandoned him just yet.

Storm clouds gather

World War One was meant to be "the war to end all wars" but trouble had been brewing in Europe since the signing of the Treaty of Versailles in 1919. Germany had been severely punished for its part in the war and had suffered from economic depression and massive unemployment ever since. Out of this misery came a political figure hell-bent on making Germany great again. Adolf Hitler

▶ *The coming storm: Adolf Hitler takes the salute at a Nazi march-past on "The Party Day of the Worker" in Nuremburg, Germany, 13 September 1937.*

(1889–1945) was an Austrian by birth who'd lived in Vienna from 1904 to 1913. It was in these years that Freud had finally found some recognition, especially in the US. Despite anti-Semitism he had also become a professor at the University of Vienna. Hitler, meanwhile had spent some of the most worthless years of his life on the streets of Vienna as a down-and-out artist. The experience had made Hitler bitter and he turned his hatred on an easy target – the Jews.

Being Jewish

Anti-Semitism had been growing in Vienna since the end of the nineteenth century, and though Freud had turned his back on his religion he abhorred prejudice against Jews. For years he had even wondered if resistance to psychoanalysis had been stronger because it was developed by a Jew. As he got older Freud began to look at his own Judaism, and believed "that I owe only to my Jewish nature the two characteristics that had become indispensable on my difficult life's way. Because I was a Jew, I found myself free from many prejudices which limited others in the employment of their intellects, and as a Jew I was prepared to

A partnership of geniuses

Freud enjoyed it when his name was paired with the great Jewish mathematical physicist Albert Einstein. The two great men shared pacifist sentiments and in the 1930s they began a correspondence, which they intended to publish. These letters about the nature of war, and how war could be prevented, were published as *Why War?* in 1933.

go into opposition."

This personal enlightenment came at a time when being Jewish was about to become life-threatening. In January 1933 Hitler, the ultimate anti-Semite, finally became chancellor of Germany. Very soon Jews were being beaten up and murdered by Hitler's Nazis, or arrested and taken to concentration camps. In May 1933 books by Jews and Marxists were piled onto bonfires throughout Germany. The works of Freud and his friend Einstein were among those burned to ashes. "What progress we are making," Freud quipped: "In the Middle Ages they would have burned me; nowadays they are content with burning my books."

▶ *A photograph from the 1920s of the physicist Albert Einstein, with whom Freud exchanged ideas.*

Some of Freud's friends urged him to leave Vienna but Freud remained confident that Hitler and his Nazis wouldn't take over Austria.

Being old and frail he believed he was beyond the clutches of the Nazis, anyway. He felt more worried for his sons Ernst and Oliver who'd lived in Berlin but later that year fled Germany. Oliver went to Vienna for a while before settling in the USA, and Ernst left for England.

Staying on in Vienna

Patients continued to come to Berggasse 19, Freud carried on writing and life in many ways seemed to go on as normal. In the summer of 1934 he was working on a fictional historical novel called *Moses and Monotheism*. This time Freud rewrote the history of the Jews by suggesting that Moses was an Egyptian priest. By falling back on psychoanalysis he also gave explanations for anti-Semitism. The crucial part of his new theory was the Jewish custom of circumcision. Freud believed that it was the non-Jew's fear of circumcision, or castration as Freud translated it, that had caused centuries of persecution. It was a far-fetched idea, but on this occasion Freud was writing fiction.

By 1935 Freud referred to Berggasse 19 as his "prison". He still worked for five hours each day but found enjoyment in reading, walking and flowers. Anna still cared for him and though he worried about her not being married he took a selfish pleasure in her company, calling her "the most enjoyable thing near me". There were other pleasures though, and in 1935 he was pleased when the Royal Society of Medicine in England named him an honorary member. It was a sign that psychoanalysis had been truly accepted in Britain, and Freud felt flattered.

In 1936 it was Freud's 80th birthday, and Martha and he celebrated their 50th wedding anniversary. By now passion had long gone but Freud remained fond of the woman who had shared his life. She had been the selfless partner who had kept his household running smoothly throughout the long years that he struggled with his science: "It was really not a bad solution of the marriage problem," he wrote of Martha, "and she is still today tender, healthy and active."

Time to flee

On 12 March 1938 Freud was listening to his radio when appalling news was

▲ *Persecution of Austrian Jews began after the Anschluss (annexation) of Austria by Germany in 1938.*

Here, Nazis humiliate Jewish people in Vienna by forcing them to wash the streets.

announced. By now his face had been so contorted by the prosthesis that he seemed to look upon the world with a permanent grimace. Today of all days he had more reason than ever to look downcast – the Nazis had finally marched into Austria.

That same day troops arrived in Vienna and Jews were immediately rounded up and attacked. Very quickly, non-Jews turned against their neighbours, and joined in with the Nazi humiliations. The scenes were terrible as old and young Jews were made to scrub away anti-Nazi graffiti, or even clean the roads. Two days later Hitler visited the capital and announced the *Anschluss* (annexation) of Austria. Most Jewish businesses closed down.

Freud saw his last patient and held the final meeting of his colleagues at Berggasse 19. He was reluctant to leave Vienna but urged the others to carry on their work abroad. Freud might well have felt an outcast most of his life but in his hour of need old friends tried to help him. Ernest Jones and Marie Bonaparte came to Vienna and pleaded with him to leave the city. An American envoy sent a telegram to the USA, saying: "Fear (that) Freud, despite age and illness, (is) in danger." This message was relayed to President Franklin D Roosevelt who made it clear to the Nazis that the US knew what was happening, a move that most probably saved Freud's life.

The Nazi police – the *Gestapo* – did however storm his house, steal his money and arrest Anna. She was interrogated for one day, which was enough to finally convince Freud that he should leave Vienna. Before the Freuds left, the Gestapo asked Freud to sign a statement agreeing that his family had not been badly treated. Freud was old, tired and depressed but his wit and sarcasm remained razor sharp. Apparently, the words, "I can most highly recommend the Gestapo to everyone" came to him but he never wrote them down.

A new life in London

Freud was too ill to travel to the USA so he settled upon London. On 4 June 1938 a frail, white-haired Freud boarded a train in Vienna with his wife, sister-in-law and daughter. They travelled to Paris and then onwards to London. They left behind four of Freud's sisters who later died in

▶ *Sigmund and Anna Freud photographed in Paris on their way to London on 5 June 1938.*

concentration camps. Not even the all-knowing father of psychoanalysis, the discoverer of the death instinct, could have foreseen their harrowing end. Nor could he have imagined the death and destruction that was about to unfold in Europe. Freud came to England "to die in freedom", but for a year he lived in relative peace and tranquillity. The family settled in Maresfield Gardens in Hampstead, a leafy village-like area of London.

Freud marvelled at the way the English took to him. He and Martha received flowers and warm wishes, and welcomed old friends like Marie Bonaparte, and new acquaintances like the author H.G. Wells and the surreal artist Salvador Dalí to Maresfield Gardens. He saw a few patients and resumed writing his novel, *Moses and Monotheism.*

"My last war"

By March 1939 the situation in Europe was becoming increasingly unstable and Hitler invaded Czechoslovakia.

Since his arrival in London Freud had tried to push the guilt he felt about his sisters in Vienna to the back of his mind. In addition, the pain in his jaw refused to go away. The cancer had returned but this time it was inoperable, and Freud, who was also suffering from a weakened heart, knew he had only months to live. In July he saw his last patient, and then it was just a matter of waiting until the end.

Germany invaded Poland on 1 September, and a few days later World War Two had begun. Within days an air-raid siren had gone off in Hampstead. When a radio broadcaster suggested this would be the "last war", Freud joked that it would be "my last war". He died on 23 September 1939 at the age of 83.

▶ *Freud and Martha in the garden at Hampstead, London, in September 1939, just before his death.*

Life after Freud

Anna Freud had been at her father's side for years. She remained with him until the end when his doctor gave him the final overdose of morphine that Freud had requested when the pain became too much to bear.

Anna missed her father terribly but she made it her life's work to protect and uphold his memory. She carried on living at Maresfield Gardens with her mother and Auntie Minna. Eventually, the house became a kind of time-warp with Freud's books, his collection of classical statuettes, even his couch draped in oriental rugs, still in place.

Minna died in 1941, but Martha survived until 1951 when she was 90 years old. By now a couple of biographies about Freud, and a collection of his letters to Wilhelm Fliess, the German ear, nose and throat specialist who had been his close friend from 1893 to 1902, had already been published. At Anna's insistence the letters had been carefully edited, as would be all material subsequently published about her father that she could influence. In 1952 Ernest Jones finished the first part of his biography of Freud. Jones remained loyal to his old friend and gave a sympathetic account of Freud's life, which breezed over aspects that Anna found uncomfortable, such as Freud's own neuroses, and his research and use of cocaine.

Anna had less control over other publications about her father. In 1974 the letters between Freud and Jung were published for the first time. Anna wanted parts of her father's letters to be censored, but it is fortunate that her wishes weren't followed as these letters give a true insight into the minds of the two great pioneers of psychoanalysis.

Anna's life

Anna never married. Instead she dedicated her life to her father's memory and her work as a child psychologist. While Freud had focused on adults, Anna sought to

▶ *Anna Freud, photographed in 1970.*

The women who outlived him

"And yet how terribly difficult it is to have to do without him. To continue to live without so much kindness and wisdom beside one! It is small comfort for me to know that in the fifty-three years of our married life not one angry word fell between us, and that I always sought as much as possible to remove from his path the misery of everyday life. Now all my life has lost all content and meaning."
Martha Freud in a letter to Ludwig Binswanger soon after her husband's death

"I miss the daily contact with him, the interchange of thought, the need he had for me, quite apart from all I needed from him. He had such a way to reduce every occurrence to its right proportions, whether it was just some daily difficulty or disappointment or a big loss, like that of home and work and security as it occurred before our emigration. There was nothing that could throw him off his balance. It is much more difficult to see things in their right light without his help."
Anna Freud writing to A.A Brill, the leader of the New York Psychoanalytic Society, soon after her father's death

deal with children whose problems were in the present, not in the dim and distant past. During the war, soon after her father's death, she set up the Hampstead War Nursery for children suffering from parental deprivation. After the war she gave courses on child psychology at Maresfield Gardens and in 1952 she set up the Hampstead Clinic, which was dedicated to improving the mental health of children. She wrote books on psychoanalysis, but most of her energy was channelled into the analysis of children, and finding ways of improving that analysis.

Anna found her theories, and those of her father, constantly under fire. Her main adversary would be Melanie Klein, the London-based psychoanalyst who had discovered her own theory and technique of child analysis. Although Klein's theories were based on those of Freud's, she believed the Oedipal stage of development came much earlier. The differences between Anna Freud and Melanie Klein almost caused a split in The British Psychoanalytical Society but eventually training courses were set up for each group.

Throughout her life Anna travelled regularly to the USA to teach and give lectures. In 1950 she collected an honorary doctorate from Clark University where her father had been honoured in 1909. As well as doctorates from Harvard University and the University of Vienna she was made a Commander of the Order of the British Empire (CBE) in Britain, a title that is given by the king or queen for good works. Anna Freud died in 1982, and the clinic that she had founded was renamed the Anna Freud Centre. In 1986 Maresfield Gardens, her home for 40 years, was turned into the Freud Museum.

▼ *The garden frontage of Freud's London home, now the Freud Museum.*

The debate

Many psychoanalysts have remained entirely loyal to Freud, or else based their own ideas and methods upon his. For this reason psychoanalysts like Melanie Klein, Karen Horney and Erich Fromm are called Freudians.

Freud has also attracted a great deal of criticism, and has been accused of being a woman-hater, a liar and a fraud. Feminists are angry with him because of his ideas about women, and theories such as penis envy. Other critics point out that some of his case studies were forced to fit his theories, and that at times his theories were more than far-fetched.

And there is always the argument that psychoanalysis is just theory and nobody can truly understand the workings of the mind. It seems that the debate about Freud and the nature of psychoanalysis will go on forever, although even the most steadfast critic has to acknowledge that Freud changed the way we look at ourselves.

The changes

In his lifetime Freud often revised his theories, so it seems predictable that psychoanalysis would continue to evolve after his death. Nowadays, psychoanalysts do not place so much emphasis upon childhood experiences, and are as likely to look at events in adulthood and current relationships when they analyze a patient. At the same time, Freud made us realize that childhood trauma could manifest itself in nervous disorders later in life. Today, parents try to understand the problems that their children are going through, rather than lose patience with them and punish them.

Most psychoanalysts agree that Freud placed too much emphasis upon sexuality in his theories, yet he opened the door to a more honest and serious discussion of sexual matters.

Now that people can talk about these matters more freely they are less likely to suffer in silence, and in turn, suffer the consequences later in life.

▶ *Freud's legacy – the science of psychoanalysis – continues to evolve and change today.*

Glossary

analyze To examine something carefully in order to understand it.

anatomist A person who has studied the structure of the human body.

anti-Semitism Hatred and prejudice against Jews.

appendicitis An illness where the appendix has become infected and needs to be surgically removed.

atheist Somebody who does not believe that there is a God.

castration Removal of the testicles so they can no longer produce sperm.

circumcision The surgical removal of the foreskin at the end of a boy's penis, normally performed shortly after birth.

complex Strong drives within yourself that make it difficult for you to feel or act normally. These feelings are often repressed.

consummate To have sexual intercourse at the beginning of a relationship or marriage.

crank An eccentric person who is obsessed by a particular theory.

dermatologist A doctor who specializes in the diagnosis and treatment of skin disorders.

disorder Another word for a minor illness or disease.

feminist Someone who believes that women should have the same opportunities and rights as men.

free association A method of investigating a person's unconscious by asking them to make spontaneous associations with words or ideas.

genitals/ genitalia (pl.) The reproductive, or sex, organs.

Gestapo The German secret police under Nazi rule.

hallucinations Something a person sees in their head that is not really there.

hysteria The physical symptoms of neurosis, which can include paralysis, headaches and sleeplessness.

inferior Describes something that is not as good as something else.

insomnia A disorder that makes sleeping difficult or impossible.

instinct Behaviour that is natural and not learned. If you feel hungry it is a natural instinct to eat.

libido A natural drive or energy in a person, usually used to describe sexual desire.

manifest To show or display something to the eye or in the mind.

masturbate To touch your own sexual organs and become aroused.

myth An ancient story or legend, usually about gods and heroes.

natural sciences The branches of science used in the study of the physical world. These include physics, chemistry, geology, biology and botany.

nervous system The series of nerves in a human body that transmit messages to the brain.

neurology The scientific study of the nervous system.

neurosis Originally described as a disease of the nerves, but came to mean the mild personality disorders that can interfere with someone's normal life.

neurotic Used to describe a person who has a neurosis.

obsession An idea or thought that dominates a person's mind and influences their behaviour.

obsessive-compulsive disorders
Obsessions are ideas that are abnormal and intrude upon a person's ability to live a normal life. Symptoms of an obsessive-compulsive disorder include performing a ritual over and over again, such as washing the hands.

panic attack A sudden and uncontrollable feeling of fear where a person's heart rate becomes raised and they think they will pass out or die.

phobia An abnormal fear of something.

physician Another word for a doctor.

prosthesis An artificial part for the body, such as a false leg.

protégé A person who is taught or protected by another person.

psyche The mind or spirit.

psychiatry The branch of medicine that treats mental illness or psychosis. Techniques include electro-shock therapy and certain drugs.

psychoanalysis The theory and therapeutic treatment of neuroses.

psychology The scientific study of the human mind or science of behaviour. Psychoanalysis is a branch of psychology.

psychosis Term for severe mental illnesses where it has become impossible for the patient to separate fantasy from reality. Psychoses include schizophrenia, manic depression and paranoia. These

illnesses cannot be cured by
psychoanalysis.

reminiscences Memories.

repress To put something to the back of
your mind, or to try to forget a part of
yourself of which you feel ashamed.

scepticism Prone to criticizing or
doubting things.

therapy The non-surgical treatment of
physical or mental disorders.

unconscious The part of the mind
where certain memories, fantasies and
desires are stored.

zoology The scientific study of animals.

Further reading

Anna Freud Elisabeth Young-Bruehl
Macmillan 1988

Freud: A Beginner's Guide Ruth Berry
Hodder and Stoughton 2000

Introducing Freud Richard Appignanesi and
Oscar Zarate
Icon Books 1999

Freud's Women Lisa Appignanesi and
John Forrester
Weidenfeld and Nicolson, London 1992

Dr Freud: A Life Paul Ferris
Sinclair Stevenson 1997

Freud: A Life for our Time Peter Gay
J M Dent and Sons 1988

Against Therapy Jeffrey Masson
Collins 1990

Why Freud Was Wrong Richard Webster
Harper Collins 1995

Freud's Footnotes Darian Leader
Faber 2000

The Freud/Jung Letters
Penguin 1991

*Cassandra's Daughters: A History of Psychoanalysis
in Europe and America* Joseph Schwarz
Allen Lane/The Penguin Press 1999

Freud on Women Elizabeth Young-Bruehl
The Hogarth Press 1990

Freud: A Very Short Introduction Anthony Storr
Oxford University Press 1989

Timeline

1856 6 May: Sigismund Scholomo Freud is born in Freiburg, Moravia (now part of Czech Republic).

1859 The Freuds move from Freiburg to Leipzig; Charles Darwin publishes *The Origin of Species*.

1860 The Freuds settle in Vienna.

1865 Freud enters Leopoldstadter Gymnasium school.

1873 Freud graduates from high school and attends University of Vienna to study medicine.

1877 Freud's first publication, on the intersexuality of eels.

1881 Freud graduates as a Doctor of Medicine from the University of Vienna; Dr Josef Breuer treats Bertha Pappenheim of the "Anna O" case.

1882 Freud becomes engaged to Martha Bernays, starts work at Vienna General Hospital.

1884 Freud publishes paper "On Coca".

1885 Freud visits the Salpêtrière Hospital in Paris to study under Professor Jean Martin Charcot.

1886 April: Freud opens his first private practice in Vienna.

13 September: Freud marries Martha Bernays.

October: Freud gives a lecture to the Viennese Physicians' Society about hysteria.

1887 October: Freud's first child, Mathilde, is born; Freud meets Dr Wilhelm Fliess; experiments with hypnotism; works with Josef Breuer on *Studies in Hysteria*.

1891 The Freuds move to Berggasse 19.

1894 Freud falls out with Dr Josef Breuer.

1895 *Studies in Hysteria* is published; Minna Bernays moves into Berggasse 19; Freud has his famous dream, "The Dream of Irma's Injection".

1896 Freud uses the term "psychoanalysis" for the first time in a paper published in France.

21 April: Freud introduces the Seduction Theory in a lecture at the Association for Psychiatry and Neurology.

23 October: Jacob, Freud's father, dies.

1897 Freud rejects the Seduction Theory; he begins a period of self-analysis, and develops theory of infantile sexuality and the Oedipus Complex.

1899 Freud completes *The Interpretation of Dreams*.

1900 Freud publishes *The Interpretation of Dreams*, falls out with Dr Wilhelm Fliess and begins work on *Psychopathology of Everyday Life*, in which he introduces the "Freudian Slip".

1902 Freud is made a professor of the University of Vienna; first meetings of the Wednesday Psychological Society at Berggasse 19.

1905 Freud publishes *Three Essays on Sexuality*; "Dora" case is published; publishes *Jokes and their Relation to the Unconscious*.

1907 3 March: Freud meets the Swiss psychoanalyst Dr Carl Gustav Jung for the first time.

October: Freud first treats Ernst Lanzer of the "Rat Man" case.

1908 April: The Wednesday Society changes its name to the Vienna Psychoanalytic Society; the first International Congress of Psychology and Neurology is held in Salzburg; Freud treats Herbert Graf of the "Little Hans" case.

1909 10 September: Freud attends Clark University, Worcester, Massachusetts, USA to collect an honorary degree.

1910 The Second International Psychoanalytic Congress is held in Nuremberg; the International Psychoanalytic Association (IPA) is formed with Dr Carl Jung as its president; Freud first treats Serge Pankejeff of the "Wolf Man" case.

1911 Freud works on *Totem and Taboo*; Adler and Stekel break away from the Vienna Society.

1912 Carl Jung publishes *The Psychology of the Unconscious*; Ferenczi suggests the formation of the "secret council".

24 November: Freud and Jung meet in Munich and Freud faints.

1913 January: Freud writes his last letter to Jung.

1914 World War One begins; Jung leaves the official psychoanalytic movement.

1918 World War One ends. Freud completes *Mourning and Melancholia*.

October: Freud begins analysis of Anna Freud.

1920 Freud's daughter Sophie dies from influenza; Freud publishes *Beyond the Pleasure Principle*; 6th International Psychoanalytic Congress is held at The Hague.

1921 Freud publishes *Group Psychology and the Analysis of the Ego*.

1923 Freud publishes *The Ego and the Id*. Freud is first diagnosed with cancer of the jaw. Freud's grandson, Heinele, dies from tuberculosis.

1924 Freud begins *An Autobiographical Study*; Freud finishes his analysis of Anna; Anna begins practising psychoanalysis.

1926 Freud is 70; Karl Abraham dies of lung cancer; Freud meets Einstein in Berlin; publishes *Inhibitions, Symptoms and Anxiety*.

1927 Freud writes *The Future of an Illusion*.

1930 Freud publishes *Civilization and its Discontents*; Freud is awarded the Goethe Prize for Literature; Amalia, Freud's mother, dies.

1932 Freud's exchange of letters with Albert Einstein is published under the title *Why War?*

1933 Adolf Hitler becomes Chancellor of Germany.

May: The Nazis burn books by Freud and other psychoanalysts in cities throughout Germany.

1934 Freud begins his fictional work, *Moses and Monotheism*.

1935 Royal Society of Medicine in England names Freud as an honorary member.

1936 Freud turns 80.

1938 March: Nazis invade Austria; Freud receives his last patients at Berggasse 19 and hosts last session of the Vienna Society.

4 June: Freud and his family leave Vienna for England.

Autumn: The Freuds settle in Hampstead in London.

1939 March: Hitler invades Czechoslavakia.

September: Hitler invades Poland; outbreak of World War Two.

23 September: Freud dies at 83.

1941 Minna Bernays dies.

1942 Freud's sister Adolphine dies in Theresienstadt transit camp; Mitzi, Rosa and Paula taken to Treblinka extermination camp.

1951 Martha Freud dies.

1952 Anna Freud establishes the Hampstead Clinic.

1982 Anna Freud dies.

Index

Page numbers in italics are pictures or maps.